HOW TO PLAY **GUITAR**
BEGINNER**COMPILATION**

The Complete Course for Beginner Guitarists. Learn Chords, Exercises and Tab

JOSEPH **ALEXANDER**

FUNDAMENTAL**CHANGES**

How To Play Guitar

The Complete Course for Beginner Guitarists. Learn Chords, Exercises and Tab

ISBN: 978-1-78933-062-5

Published by **www.fundamental-changes.com**

www.fundamental-changes.com

Twitter: @guitar_joseph

Over 10,000 fans on Facebook: **FundamentalChangesInGuitar**

Instagram: **FundamentalChanges**

For over 350 Free Guitar Lessons with Videos Check Out

www.fundamental-changes.com

Cover Image Copyright: Adobe Stock

With huge thanks to Levi Clay and Pete Sklaroff for all their hard work making this project happen

Other Beginner Guitar Books from Fundamental Changes

Beginner Lead Guitar Method

Beginner's Guitar Lessons: The Essential Guide

Country Guitar for Beginners

First Chord Progressions for Guitar

Guitar Chords in Context

The Beginner's Guitar Method Compilation

Contents

Book 3: The First 100 Guitar Exercises for Beginners   145

Introduction to The Compilation

Welcome to the most comprehensive, fun and *musical* beginner's guide to playing guitar.

I've been writing books on playing the guitar for nearly seven years now, and in that time Fundamental Changes has become one of the biggest music tuition publishing houses in the world. In fact, in the last few years we've sold around *half a million books*. Recently, we've teamed up with some of the best guitarists on the planet, such as jazz giant, Martin Taylor MBE, rock virtuoso Chris Brooks and country picker Levi Clay.

Between us, we've written and published nearly 100 music books, many of which have been Amazon best sellers.

One thing that concerns us all is the number of low-quality eBooks that wannabe teachers are self-publishing on Amazon. A few are great, but many of them are written by faceless guitarists with no background at all in music. Not only are some of them poorly written, many of them contain potentially harmful information for the beginning guitarist, sending them down the wrong path and causing bad habits that will take years to fix once they've taken root.

We thought it'd be a great idea for the Fundamental Changes teachers to collect together their favourite exercises for to beginner guitarists and help to cut through the damaging misinformation out there.

That collection of exercises and advice became **The First 100 Guitar Exercises for Beginners** and is the third book in this compilation. It teaches you what to play, how to play it, and more importantly *why* you should practise these skills to become a better guitarist. You'll discover a healthy approached to practice that'll set you up for a productive and musical future as a funky, groovy, rocky, sexy guitarist!

You'll develop finger independence, speed, strength, stamina and great feel on the guitar if you follow our instructions and incorporate the exercises as part of a balanced diet of learning songs, listening to music and exploring the music you love. The exercises are designed to support your studies and help you conquer the common playing problems that beginners encounter.

So that's book three, but what else will you find in this compilation?

Well, the first thing you need to understand before you can play a note is how guitar music is written down in *tablature*. Form the very basics, right through to advanced techniques like tapping, harmonics and beyond, **How to Read Guitar Tablature** will take you on a journey of discovery and teach you to write, play and *apply* every technique in modern guitar playing.

While How to Read Guitar Tablature works as a stand-alone book, it's also an essential reference guide. If you need to play or write down a new technique this is your de-facto resource. Each technique is described in detail, and there are some cool examples to show you how they're used in real music. As a beginner, you should work through it to learn about techniques you've not seen before. However, as you work through other books and learn new music, How to Read Guitar Tablature will be your go to reference guide on the right way to play.

Book Two in the compilation is my constantly best-selling title **The First 100 Chords for Guitar**. In it you'll find a complete method to learning the most important guitar chords, connecting them together and actually making music with chords. You'll discover strumming patterns, healthy practice habits, and plenty of useful chord progressions to get you writing your own songs quickly.

The First 100 Chords for Guitar is loosely based around the first twenty chord lessons I give to new beginner students, and will develop your skills from zero to hero on the guitar in a couple of weeks. You'll learn how to confidently place your fingers on the guitar, move between chords, stay in time with the music and strum the guitar like a pro in no time. It's a proven method and I know you're going to love it.

One thing you might notice, due to this being a compilation of three guitar books is that occasionally some information is briefly repeated. For example, I recap some of the How to Read Guitar Tab information at the beginning of The First 100 Exercises for Beginners. Also, some of the beginner strumming exercises in First 100 Chords form the basis of a small chunk of the exercises book. I asked myself whether I should edit these out of the compilation, but it felt better to include them as a recap is always good. This isn't the kind of book you should read sequentially. Instead you'll dip in and out of the parts that interest you, so I've deliberately allowed the same information to be repeated in case you miss it the first time around.

If you can already play a little bit and understand guitar tablature, then have a quick flick through How to Read Guitar Tablature and make sure you're up to speed with the basics in the first few chapters. Then, work through First 100 Chords and First 100 Exercises together as part of your daily practice routine. If you have 30 minutes planned for your session, spend about 10-15 minutes working on First Chords, and no more than 5 minutes working on First Exercises. You remaining time should be spend on learning *actual music*. Try to find a song you like and begin learning it as soon as possible. This way, you'll learn to pick exercises from the book that compliment your progress as a guitarist.

Throughout, there are tips on how to practise to get the most from your sessions, advise on how to improve quickly and most importantly how to stay healthy and positive when learning the guitar. The tips that went into this book have been taken from a combined teaching experience of over 300 years! We've walked the road you're about to set foot on, and it's a lot of fun if you get the right advice.

My final parting shot is to keep it musical. Don't learn exercises for exercises' sake. Learn chords and songs, discover your weaknesses, then use the exercises in book three to improve the weaknesses you recognise.

Have fun and enjoy your journey. The destination is yours to find.

Joseph

P.S. go and download your audio files now from **www.fundamental-changes.com**. They'll make the book come alive and you'll 10x your progress. You need to *hear* what the music should sound like if you're going to get it right!

How to Read Guitar Tablature

A Complete Guide to Reading Guitar Tab and Performing Modern Guitar Techniques

Published by **www.fundamental-changes.com**

Twitter: **@guitar_joseph**

Over 10,000 fans on Facebook: **FundamentalChangesInGuitar**

Instagram: **FundamentalChanges**

For over 350 Free Guitar Lessons with Videos Check Out

www.fundamental-changes.com

Introduction

In one form or another, tablature has been around since the 15th century when it was used to quickly notate music for the lute. While tablature (tab) has evolved somewhat, it still looks remarkably like the first instances that were recorded over 600 years ago.

Traditional music notation uses a system of five lines and dots to describe the pitch of a note. For example, the scale of C Major looks like this when written in traditional (standard) notation.

While tablature looks similar to traditional notation in some ways, the lines now represent the six physical strings of the instrument and the dots have been replaced by numbers. These numbers tell us which fret to play on which string of the instrument. The scale of C Major above can be written on guitar as follows.

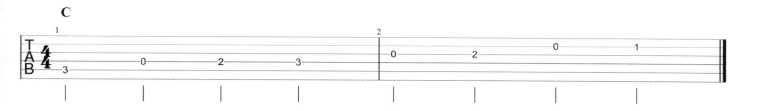

The notes in the previous two diagrams are identical.

So why, when there's a perfectly good system of traditional music notation available, do guitarists prefer to read tab?

Well, the short answer is, "Because it's much easier to read!"

On a 24-fret guitar, there are up to six locations to play the pitch E that occurs when you pick the high E string. The identical pitch can be played in the following six locations.

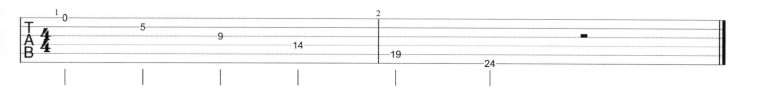

Where do I play that note?

If you play each one, you will hear that the pitch stays the same, while the *tone* of the note changes.

Most pitches on the guitar can be played in three or four different locations, which puts the guitarist at an immediate disadvantage when it comes to reading music. Each pitch on a piano can be played in only one location, so when a pianist sees a piece of traditional notation, they know what each dot means and which key they should press. Guitarists, on the other hand, need to figure out the best position to play a phrase or lick, so some trial and error may be required.

Tablature overcomes this, because it tells us instantly not only what note to play, but *where to play it*.

Tablature also has the advantage of being immediately accessible to read for a beginner. That's why most guitarists prefer to read tab so much more than they prefer to read music.

If, on your very first guitar lesson, I were to teach you via traditional music notation, I would first have to show you what note each line and space represented. You'd have to learn what those notes were and memorise them. Then you'd have to learn and memorise the location of those notes on the guitar neck.

Finally, you'd have to "decode" the series of dots I wrote down for you, figure out which notes they were, find them on the guitar and then play them. It's quite an undertaking! I've not even started talking about rhythm yet, and if I were to write a chord there could be up to six dots stacked on top of each other!

Using tab, however, I can quickly show you that the bottom line represents the low E bass string and the top line is the high E string, and that the numbers written on each string tell you which fret to play; no decoding necessary. Then we can get on with the important business of making music and rocking out!

Don't get me wrong, reading traditional notation is a vital skill for every musician to master, and you should make every effort to learn, but it's certainly not a goal for your first guitar lesson.

Adding expression

Another huge advantage of tab relates to how guitarists play the instrument. Almost every note we play tends to be embellished in some way. To move between notes we can bend, slide, tap, hammer-on, or pull-off. We add almost constant vibrato and special effects too.

When you consider that there are multiple ways to bend a note or add vibrato, then it's easy to see why traditional music is a bit clunky when it comes to notating all the nuances of guitar playing. It's so much easier to simply *draw* the desired manipulation of a bend or whammy bar trick in tab than it is to try to notate it traditionally.

As you can see, tab offers immediacy and subtlety in its notation of modern music, so reading it is an *essential skill* to master for every guitarist.

Even so, it is normal for tab to be combined with traditional notation because there is one thing that tab doesn't tell us – rhythm. It's all very well seeing a fret number on a string, but how long should you play that note for?

Providing the traditional notation in the same *system* as the tab is common. Not only because some guitarists prefer to read music than tab, but because traditional music is very good at describing how long a note should be played.

While some decent hybrids of tab exist that incorporate the rhythmic aspect of standard notation, it is far more common to see both tab and standard notation written together. Generally, there will be no rhythmic information on the tab part, so as to keep it clean and easy to read. Instead, it is contained in the standard notation line. For example:

You will learn how to read rhythm later in this book and be fully prepared to play whatever life throws at you.

For now, let's get going and get to grips with the basics of reading tab. We'll begin with a look at the lines, numbers and rhythmic symbols that tell us how the music should sound, and where it should be played on the guitar neck.

Get the Audio

The audio files for this book are available to download for free from **www.fundamental-changes.com.** The "Download Audio" link is on the menu at the top right. Click the type of book you've bought (guitar, bass etc). This will take you to a form page where you'll select the title of your book from the drop-down list. Follow the instructions to get the audio.

We recommend that you download the files directly to your computer, not to your tablet, then extract them before adding them to your media library. You can then put them onto your tablet, iPod or burn them to CD. On the download page there is a help PDF and we also provide technical support via the contact form.

Get the audio now from

www.fundamental-changes.com

Twitter: **@guitar_joseph**

Over 10,000 fans on Facebook: **FundamentalChangesInGuitar**

Instagram: **FundamentalChanges**

Chapter One: The Basics – Lines, Numbers and Rhythm

As I described in the introduction, the basics of reading tab are very simple. The tablature *stave* or *staff* contains six lines and each line represents one string of the guitar.

The easiest way to tell which one is which is to remember that the lowest (bass) string of the guitar is the lowest written line of tab. If you lay the book flat on a table, the closest line to you is the closest string to you.

The highest pitched string of the guitar (high E) is the highest line on the tab. On paper, it's the furthest line away from you and also the furthest string away from you on the guitar.

You can now easily see how the lines relate to the strings on the guitar. Often in guitar tab you will see the note names of the strings written to the left of the tab stave, and the word TAB written on the strings themselves.

Another handy way to remember which string is which is to look at the word TAB and see that the B (for bass) is on the lowest line and the T (for treble is on the highest line)

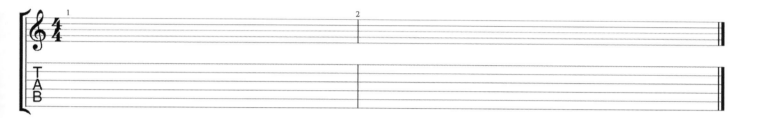

As with standard notation and written English, we read music from left to right.

To indicate that a specific fret should be played on a particular string, we simply write the required fret number on the relevant line.

Example 1a tells you to,

Play the 3rd fret on the lowest (sixth) string.

Play the 5th fret on the highest (first) string.

Play the 2nd fret on the second (B) string.

Play the 7th fret on the fourth (D) string.

Play through the following example and listen to the audio track to check you're doing it right.

Example 1a

To indicate that a string should be played *open* without any fretted note, we simply write a 0 on the required string.

Example 1b

If we need to play two or more notes at once, the fret numbers are stacked vertically on top of each other. Remember, we read from left to right, so notes that are written vertically are played simultaneously. Pick or strum the following example.

Example 1c

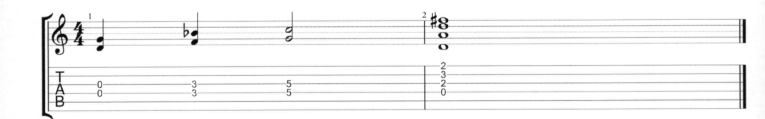

In the previous example, you may have recognised the final chord of D Major. Normally, when a full chord is notated in tablature we add the chord grid and symbol above it to make the music easier to read.

Example 1d

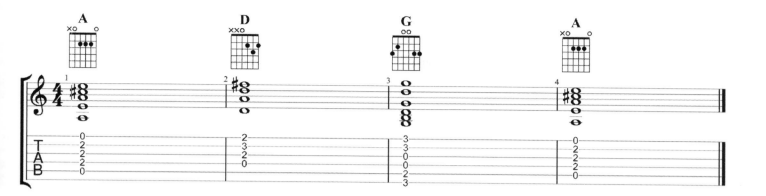

To test yourself, play the following melody on your guitar.

Example 1e

Finally, it's possible to play a note on the guitar which doesn't have any pitch at all. This is called a mute and it's normally performed in one of two ways.

The first way is to gently press on the string with the fretting hand, making sure you don't push the string all the way down to the fret.

The second way is to mute the string as you play it with your fretting hand.

When you pick a muted note it should sound dead and percussive. It definitely shouldn't sustain.

Single notes and whole chords can be muted.

However you play it, a muted note is shown by an X on the string instead of a number.

Example 1f

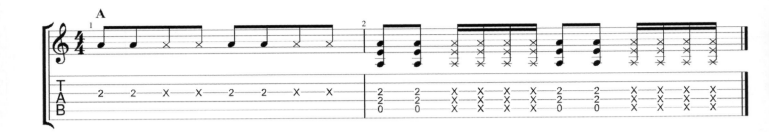

Reading Rhythm

Some people consider that the way guitar tab deals with rhythm to be a bit of a failure. I couldn't disagree more. In fact, when combined with traditional music notation, tab is a fantastic way to show both when to play a note and how long it lasts for.

Rhythmically, that hardest tab to read is the stuff you might find online in places like **www.ultimate-guitar. com**. With these "ASCII" style tabs, rhythm is shown by how the notes are spaced out on the line. No actual rhythm notation is given.

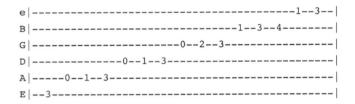

While this kind of works if the rhythm is straightforward, anything more complex than simple 1/8th or 1/16th notes can be hard to decipher.

Another evolution of tab combines the rhythm notation with the tab in one stave. Rhythm values are added above the tab line and, as long as you understand how rhythms are written on the guitar, you'll know when to play each note.

You may see something like the example below. Don't worry! You don't have to play this… yet!

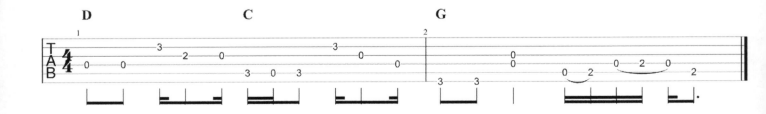

Let's take a quick look at how to read rhythm notation, so you'll be well prepared when you see it out in the wild.

In written music, rhythm is broken down into *bars* (or *measures*) that contain *beats*.

Bars are containers that normally contain four beats. Each beat is split into rhythms that are named according to how they divide a standard bar of four beats.

Special markings are used to tell you how long a note should last for.

For example,

- A whole note fills one whole bar

- A 1/2 note fills half the bar (there are two half notes into one bar)

- There are four 1/4 notes in a bar

- There are eight 1/8th note in a bar

- There are sixteen 1/16th notes in a bar

These notes are written in the following way:

Underneath each note I have shown its equivalent *rest* value. A rest lasts the same amount of time as a note that has a pitch, however it indicates that there should be silence for the allotted time.

Notice that 1/8th notes and 1/16th notes have *flags* joining them together. 1/8th notes have one flag and 1/16th notes have two flags. Each time you add a flag the length of each note halves, so a 1/32nd note would have three flags.

Every piece of music begins with a time signature which tells you how many beats there are in a bar. The most common time signature in music is 4/4, which tells you that there are four 1/4 notes in each bar. (We'll take a look at rhythmic values in a minute).

Other common time signatures are 3/4 (three 1/4 note beats in a bar) and 12/8 (twelve 1/8th notes in a bar, arranged 1 2 3 1 2 3 1 2 3 1 2 3). 12/8 is the time signature of most blues tunes.

In the UK, there is a different system for naming note lengths:

A whole note = a semibreve

A 1/2 note = a minim

A 1/4 note = a crotchet

A 1/8th note = a quaver

A 1/16th note = a semiquaver

This may seem strange to much of the rest of the world, but our system does have one big advantage compared to the international system: the metric note names of the US system are all based on the premise that there are four beats in every bar.

However, music isn't always written in 4/4 time (four beats in the bar) – you can have 3/4 time, 6/8 time or even 17/16 time. In anything other than 4/4 time there are not four 1/4 notes in the bar.

The US system does, however, work very well if we ignore this pedantic fact. It is modern, logical, easier to remember and doesn't involve learning quaint English words!

When 1/8th notes and 1/16th notes are combined, we join their tails together. Play or clap through the following rhythms. You can hear them on the audio tracks so listen as you play.

Example 1g

Note Groupings

1/8th notes and 1/16th notes can be grouped in any mathematical combination as long as we don't exceed a total of four 1/16th notes in a beat. They can be grouped in the following ways.

Example 1h

Tap your foot with a metronome and learn to recognise and *feel* the sound and effect of these rhythms.

Any of the notes in the above examples can be replaced with a corresponding rest value.

Tied Rhythms

It is possible to *tie* two notes together. When you see a tied note, you do not play the second note in the grouping. The first note is held for the value of the second note in addition to its own.

In written music, it is the convention to always leave a space between beats two and three for ease of reading. For example, you shouldn't really see this (although occasionally you will):

The above rhythm should really be written like this:

The previous two examples sound identical, but the second example is written correctly as it uses a tie to clearly show where the middle of the bar is.

If we can show the gap between one beat and another then it is normally easier to read. I would prefer to see this…

…rather than this…

Example 1i

…because, once again, the gaps between beats are shown. This is a matter of personal preference and the notation shown in the second line is often used.

Try clapping through this example that uses tied 1/16th notes.

Example 1j

Dotted Rhythms

You will often see a small dot written after a note. The dot is a rhythmic instruction to *add half of the note value again.*

For example, if we have a note that lasts for 2 beats, and we add half of the original note value again (half of 2 = 1), we end up with a note that lasts three beats.

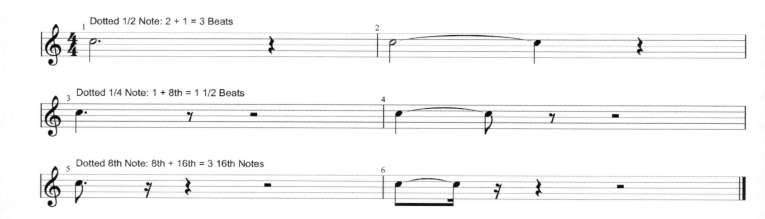

In each of the above examples you can see how adding a dot to a note value affects its length. In the second bar of each line you can see how adding a dot is mathematically the same as tying the original note to one half of its length.

Normally, the note after the dotted note will make the dotted note "add up" to a whole number of beats. For example:

Example 1k

Triplets

A triplet is simply three notes squeezed evenly into the space of two notes. They are written in a group with the number "3" above them.

When learning 1/8th note triplets it can help to say "trip-er-let trip-er-let" out loud, in time with the metronome. Make sure each "trip" coincides accurately with the metronome click. The top line in each example shows the triplet; the bottom line is just there for reference and shows where the original note value lies.

I could write a whole book on rhythms for guitar (in fact, check out my book *Sight Reading Mastery for Guitar* where I stole these examples from), but it's a bit of a rabbit hole and we've covered most of the rhythms you'll come across in modern guitar playing.

So how does all this look in tablature?

When rhythm notation is combined with tablature into one *system* (line), the note heads are removed and the remaining stems float above each note in the tab.

For example, here's a simple example that combines 1/4, 1/8th and 1/16th notes.

Example 1l

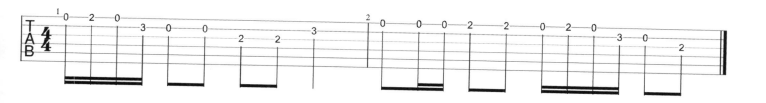

Here's a slightly more complex example that introduces a triplet and a dotted note.

Example 1m

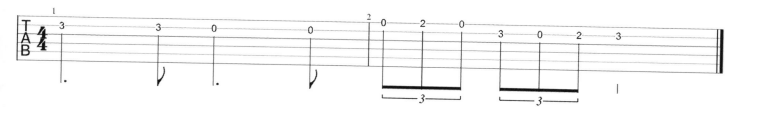

Combining tab and notation into a single line is certainly a great way to save space and clearly shows the rhythmic phrasing of each note. It's certainly a step up from the ASCII-style tab shown earlier.

However, in professional publications, you will normally see both the tablature *and* the traditional notation joined together into one line. When this happens, all the rhythmic information is included in the notation part only.

While it may seem strange to split your focus between two lines of music, this is actually a far better system than the combined tab + rhythm staff.

First, this system appeals to guitarists who don't read tab, but more importantly it allows us to cleanly add much more information to the score. This information may include things like right-hand picking, left-hand fingering, tempo, performance directions and positional information.

Here's a short example of the combined score for guitarists. Notice that the rhythm is included on the notation part and the tab part is "clean". The rhythmic spacing of notes in the tab part directly aligns with the rhythmic spacing of the notation.

Example 1n

Now you've mastered the basics of reading guitar tab and rhythm, let's get to grips with some of the special techniques used by guitarists to create expressive music. We'll start with one of the most expressive techniques on the guitar – bends.

Chapter Two: Bends

One of the most common and unique techniques used by guitar players is the bend. Bends are a great way to change pitch smoothly between a lower and a higher note. To execute a bend, you need to physically bend the string up in pitch by pushing it up the fretboard.

The amount you bend the note can be anything from less than a semitone, right up to two or more tones. The further you bend the string the higher the pitch becomes.

In tab, a bend is shown by curved line with an arrow. In the following example the note on the 7th fret of the third string (D) is bent up one tone, until it sounds exactly like the note on the 9th fret (E).

The word "full" is written above the bend to indicate that the note should be raised by a full tone.

Example 2a

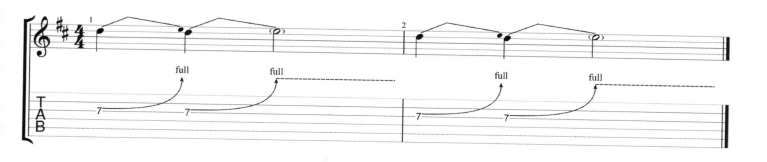

The easiest way to learn to bend is by using your third finger to fret the note and supporting it with the first and second fingers, lined up on the string behind for added strength and control. Placing three fingers on the string is much stronger than using just one.

The distance you need to bend the note is always written above the arrow. Other common distances are a 1/2 tone (semitone):

Example 2b

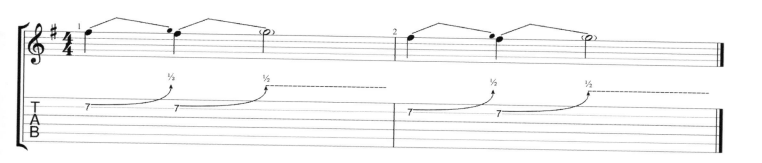

A tone and a half:

Example 2c

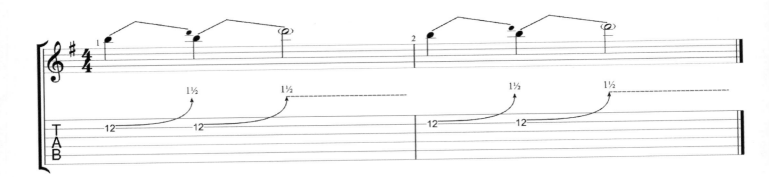

Or maybe even a 1/4 tone. This is known as a curl.

Example 2d

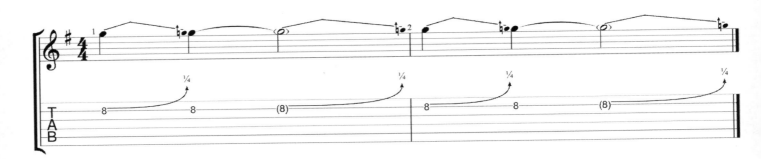

You can finish a bend in various ways. So far, I've notated bends that ascend and you don't hear them descend back to the initial note. If the bend should be held as you move your fingers back to the original pitch, another arrow is added to show this.

Example 2e

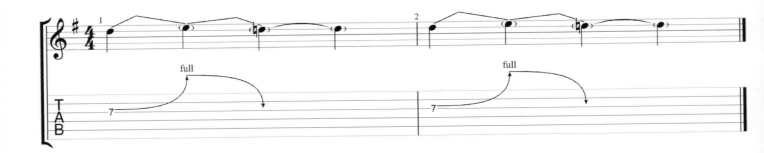

Bent notes can be held indefinitely. This bend lasts for a whole bar.

Example 2f

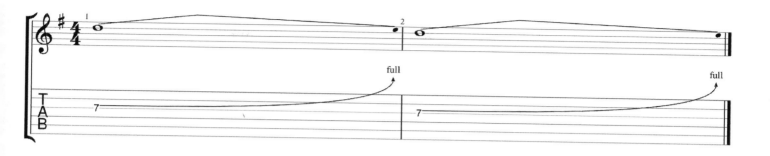

It's also important to know that you can control the amount of time it takes to reach the desired pitch. You could bend the starting note to pitch very quickly, very slowly, or anywhere in between.

In the following example, the note D (7th fret on the 3rd string) is bent up to E three times. The first time, the pitch is reached instantly. Next, the note is bent up more slowly and takes two beats to reach its target pitch. Finally, the note is bent very slowly and takes four beats to reach its destination.

As you might expect, the tab shows these nuances with the shape of the bend lines.

Example 2g

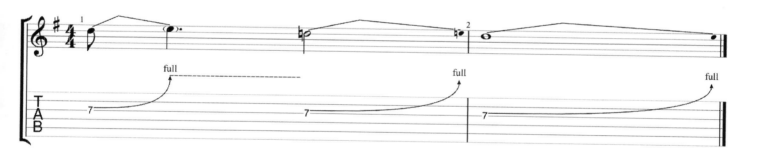

One of the unique characteristics of the guitar is that you can manipulate a note's pitch more than once after you've played it. The following example begins on the note B with a big, one-and-a-half tone bend that returns to the original pitch before being bent up a whole tone and finally returning to the starting note.

Example 2h

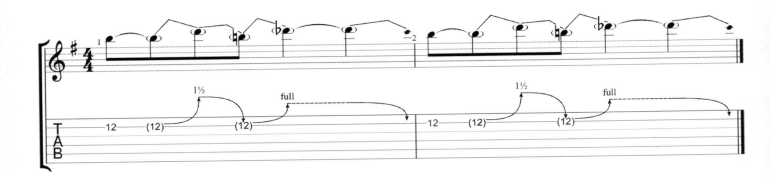

While the previous example was executed with just one pick, it is possible to pick repeatedly as you manipulate a bend. In the next example, I bend up one-and-a-half tones again, but this time I repeatedly pick the string as I slowly return the note to its starting point.

Example 2i

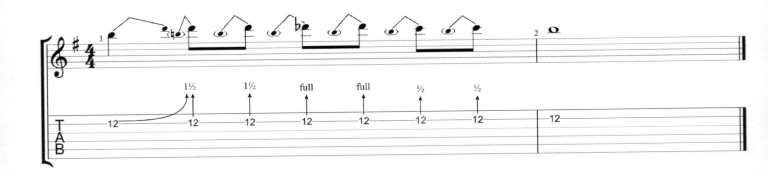

It's possible to bend a note on one string and hold it while you play another note on a higher string, as the following short country lick demonstrates.

Example 2j

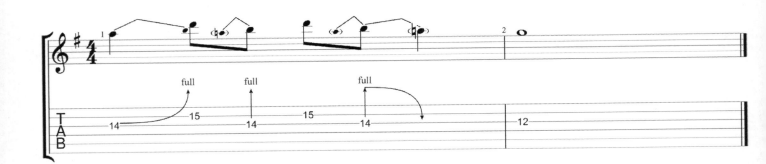

Finally, an important technique to know about is the *pre-bend*. When performing a pre-bend, you must bend the string up to the pitch required *before* picking the note. Obviously, this is quite a challenge because you have no audible reference. There are various exercises you can use to increase your skills in this area, and I detail them in my book *Complete Technique for Modern Guitar.*

The distance you should pre-bend is written above the bend arrow. The following example demonstrates the tab symbol for a pre-bend and you should bend the note by a whole tone before picking it.

Example 2k

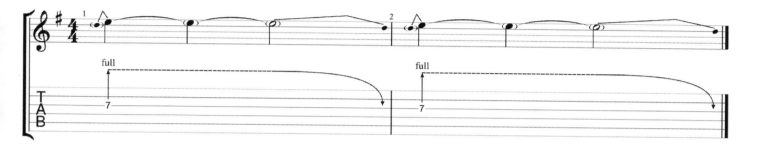

As you can see, there are many ways to play bends, but the information in this chapter should arm you to read and understand any tablature you come across on your path as a musician.

Vibrato

Vibrato is one of the most expressive techniques in music and should be an essential part of your vocabulary. Vibrato is created by performing a series of very small bends after a note has been struck. The further you bend the string, the *wider* the vibrato will be. The quicker you bend the string, the *faster* the vibrato will be.

Vibrato can be any combination of slow, fast, wide or *narrow*, and is an incredibly personal technique for a musician. Often, when learning music performed by other people you will want to copy the guitarist's vibrato, but when you are improvising on your own you should let your own vibrato shine through.

In tab and standard notation, vibrato is shown by a horizontal wavy line after the note. A wide, heavy line shows wide vibrato and a narrow line shows narrow vibrato. Listen to the audio example and look at the tab. Notice how the vibrato differs on the following two notes.

Example 21

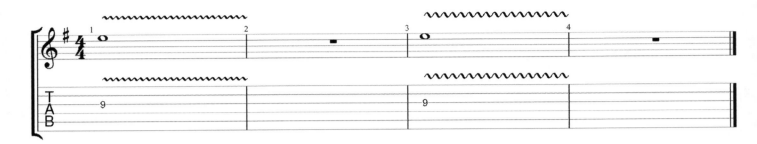

One thing to pay attention to in music is the delay before vibrato is added to a note. Sometimes the vibrato is added immediately after the note is struck, sometimes the note is held for a few beats before the vibrato is introduced. Some writers will show this by leaving a space before adding the vibrato line.

Chapter Three: Picking

Right-handed guitarists pick the guitar strings with their right hand. Most electric guitarists use a *pick* (or *plectrum*) to strike the strings and there are some important signs you need to know.

There are only two directions in which we can strike the string with the pick: Down and Up.

The symbol for a down pick looks a little like a small letter "n".

Example 3a

The symbol for an up pick looks like a letter "v".

Example 3b

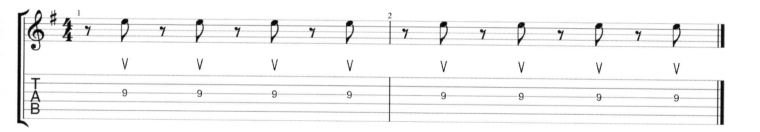

Beginners are often confused as to why the downward pointing V means up stroke. Well, look at which direction the V points in relation to the tablature. It's pointing toward the bass end of the guitar, the same direction your pick must move to perform an up pick.

Incidentally, the up and down pick notation is actually borrowed from violin music and is used to tell violinists which direction to bow their notes. The squared "n" looks like the *frog* (square end) of the bow and the "v" looks like the pointed tip of the bow.

Up and down picks are often notated to help you pick a rhythm on guitar correctly, as guitarists often use patterns of up and down picks to play a rhythm in time.

For example, this rhythm would normally be picked "down down up".

Example 3c

Whereas the following rhythm would be picked "down up up".

Example 3d

Long picking patterns occur regularly in both funk and rock, and the secret to mastering them is to isolate them and learn them one beat at a time.

Listen to the audio and see if you can master the following rhythm

Example 3e

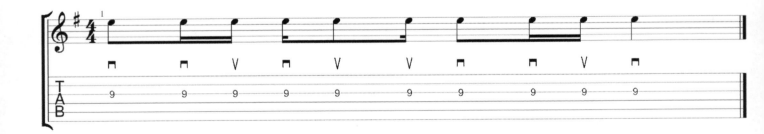

Strums

Strumming directions on guitar aren't necessarily notated in the tab part, but a good rule is that when playing chords in pop and rock, any chord that falls on the beat is played with a down strum. Any chord that's played on the *off beat* (between the beats) is played with an up strum.

So a sequence of 1/4 note chord would be played with down strums.

NB: In the following examples I've used picking directions to show the direction of the strums, but in simple music like this they probably won't be given.

Example 3f

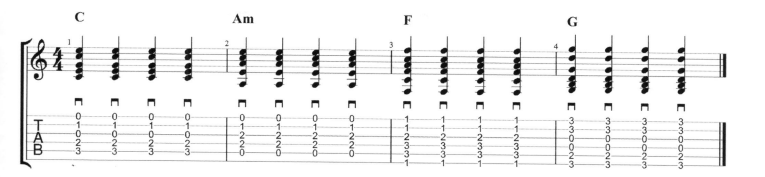

A series of 1/8th note strums would be played with both down and up strums.

Example 3g

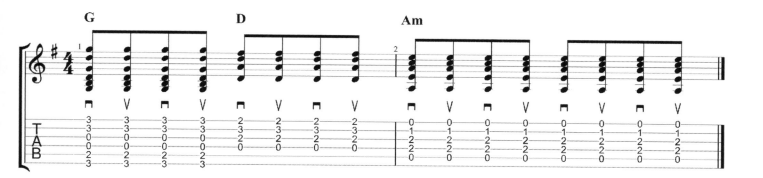

A combination of 1/4 and 1/8th note rhythms should be constructed with "units" of the previous two strumming ideas.

Of course, you don't have to use a pick to strike the string, you can also use your fingers. As a right-handed player, you use the fingers of the right hand to pick the strings while fretting notes with your left.

Each finger in the right hand is given a name which is then abbreviated and shown on the standard notation stave to show which fingers to pick with. As with many things in guitar, the names of the fingers are taken from the original Spanish.

Thumb (**P**ulgar)

Index (**I**ndice)

Middle (**M**edio)

Ring (**A**nular)

The pinkie is rarely used when finger picking.

Depending on the style of music you play, the picking thumb will function in one of two ways.

In classical music, the thumb normally takes care of any note played on the bottom three strings.

The following chord sequence uses the thumb and three fingers of the picking hand in a classical style. The thumb plays the bass note and the fingers arpeggiate through the higher notes of the chord.

Notice how the letter names for each finger are written in the notation part, but not in the tablature part.

Example 3h

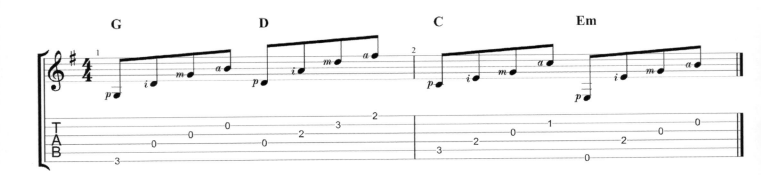

In early blues, country and folk music, the thumb often plays an alternating bassline. Below are two common patterns. The first moves between the sixth and fourth strings, while the spare picking fingers play a melody or strum a chord.

Take a quick look at the notation part. Do you see how each of the thumb picks has a downward facing stem, while the picked notes have upward facing stems? This makes the music easier to decipher.

Example 3i

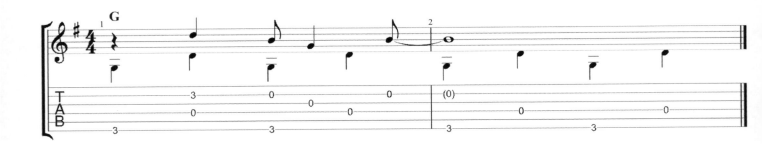

In the second common pattern, the thumb adds a note on the fifth string and moves between the sixth, fourth, fifth and fourth strings.

Example 3j

Picking Special Effects

While we are on the subject of picking, this seems to be a good time to introduce a few common and not-so-common techniques that can be performed with either the pick or the fingers.

The first is the *rake*. In its simplest form, a rake is just a slow strum through a chord. In tablature, it's shown by a thin wavy line. A rake can be played either ascending or descending. This is shown by an arrow pointing in the direction of the strum. The idea is to play the chord very slightly slower than normal, so you can hear every note in the chord.

Example 3k

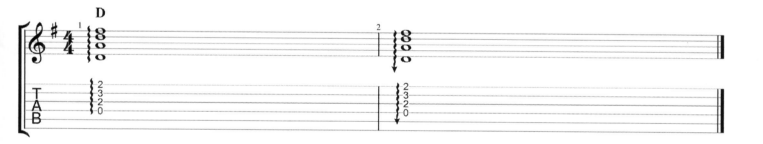

Another type of rake is the *muted rake*. This is more of a lead guitar technique and normally the final note of the rake will sound after the preceding raked notes are muted by the picking hand. While this can be performed while holding down a chord shape, its more normal to rake through an arpeggio with one note placed on each string.

Example 3l

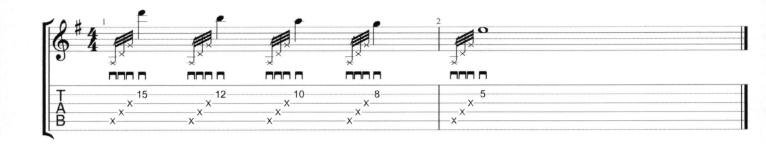

Sweep picking is a technique that's a bit like a rake and where individual notes are played on adjacent strings in a smooth, strum-like movement. Unlike a raked chord, the notes shouldn't ring into each other.

While there's no specific notation for a sweep, the clue is written in the picking directions. If you see a series of notes written one-per-string and all the picks go in one direction, it's likely to be a sweep. The following example shows a swept A Minor arpeggio played both ascending and descending. There are two notes on the top string and the picking directions are shown blow.

Example 3m

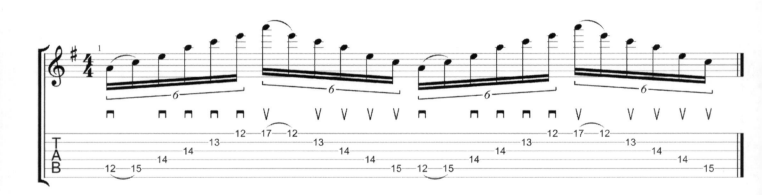

Sweep picking is a fairly advanced technique and is covered in great detail in our book, *Sweep Picking Speed Strategies for Guitar.*

Tremolo picking is the technique of quickly repeating the same note multiple times in a set rhythm. Normally it is a very fast technique and difficult to execute cleanly. In tablature and notation it is often notated using diagonal slashes through the stem of a note. Each diagonal line corresponds with the "flag" of a shorter value rhythm.

In the following example, bar one shows a 1/2 note with one slash, which corresponds to the flag of an 1/8th note, so the tremolo picking should be performed for two beats in 1/8th notes.

Bar two shows a 1/2 note with two slashes, so the tremolo picking should be played as 1/16th notes for two beats.

Bar three shows a 1/4 note with three slashes, so the tremolo should be played as 1/32nd notes for one beat.

Bar four shows a whole note with two slashes, so the tremolo should be played as 1/16th notes for four beats.

Example 3n

The difficulty of the tremolo depends very much on the tempo of the track. 1/16th note tremolos at 80bpm are fairly pedestrian, while 1/32nd notes at 120bpm are very fast indeed!

Often, three tremolo slashes through a note is simply interpreted as, *tremolo pick as fast as possible*!

The *pick slide* or *pick scrape* is more of a percussive effect than a specific picking technique and is common in most forms of hard rock. The idea is simply to slide the long side of the pick down the strings to create a grinding noise. This works much better if you use the fretting hand to mute the string and play with loads of distortion.

A pick slide can be one long movement or broken up by bouncing the edge of the pick along the strings. Either way, the tablature will show a muted note followed by a wavy line in the direction of the slide.

Example 3o

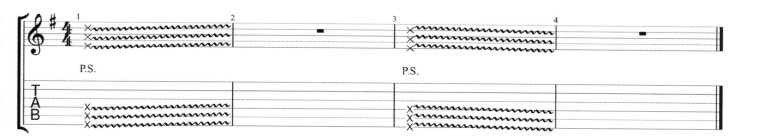

Chapter Four: Slides

Sliding is a common way to change between two notes on the guitar. The idea is that you pick one fretted note and keep the pressure on the string with your finger as you slide up (or down) to the following pitch.

There are various different ways to slide notes and they all create subtly different effects. All slides are notated by a diagonal line, but there are various was of distinguishing the different techniques.

The easiest slide to play is the *legato slide*.

To play a legato slide, pick the first note and slide to the second *without* picking the string a second time. The notation for a legato slide is a diagonal (ascending or descending) line with a *slur* written above the line.

To play a legato slide, pick the first note then slide up to the second note without picking again. The first note should be held for its full rhythmic value, so there is a definite feeling of playing both pitches evenly.

Example 4a

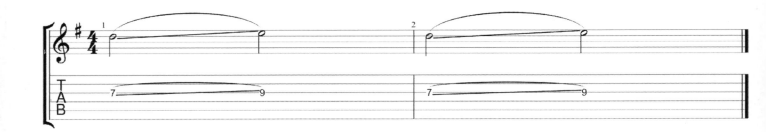

Legato slides can also be played descending.

Example 4b

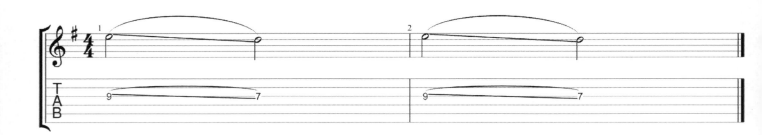

Of course, it's possible to pick the second note in the slide as well as the first. The tab notation for this slide is simply a diagonal line between the two notes, without the slur mark over the top.

In the following example, pick the 7th fret, hold the note for two beats, and slide up to the 9th fret. Just as you reach the 9th fret, pick the string again to articulate the second note. I've shown both the ascending and descending slides.

Example 4c

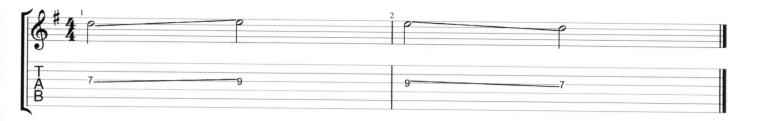

When guitarists solo, they often find ways to slightly decorate every note. A common technique is to slide quickly into a target note from an unspecified point below the pitch. This is called a *grace note slide*. The slide distance can be long or short – the important thing is to reach the target pitch in time.

In tab we show a grace note slide with a short diagonal line before the target note.

An ascending slide is notated with a /

A descending slide is notated with a \

The distance you slide is often a matter of taste and musical context.

Example 4d

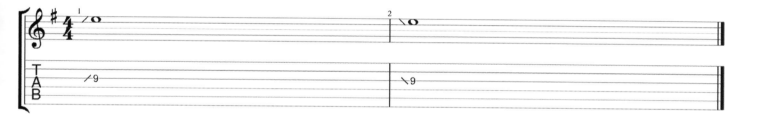

If you slide slowly up the guitar neck and keep the pressure on the string you will hear every note as you pass over the fret wire. This effect is called a *glissando* and is shown with a line between two notes.

Example 4e

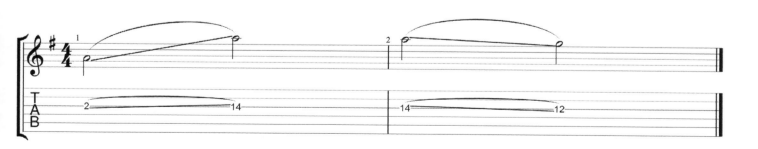

Chapter Five: Legato (Hammer-ons, Pull-offs and Taps)

Legato literally means "in a smooth and flowing manner" and on guitar this is a catch-all term for using hammer-ons, pull-offs, and even right-hand tapping. Hitting the string with the pick creates an audible sharp "attack" at the beginning of the note, so legato is any technique whereby you *don't* use the pick to sound a note.

When playing guitar, legato techniques are often used to play very quickly. Many guitarists find that the biggest factor limiting their speed and fluency is the pick. By removing most of the picked notes, it's possible to play long, smooth phrases on the guitar at breakneck speed. Joe Satriani is a huge fan of legato playing.

Let's examine the two main techniques that create legato on the guitar: hammer-ons and pull-offs.

Hammer-ons

A hammer-on is performed by picking a note then hammering a finger onto a note on the same string that's higher in pitch. The sign for a hammer-on is a short, curved line called a *slur* between the lower and higher pitched notes. You'll sometimes see the annotation "H/O" written above the line, but not always, so often you need to pay attention to the markings on the tab.

To perform the following hammer-on, use your first finger to play the 7th fret on the third string. Pick the note normally and hammer your *third* finger down onto the 9th fret *without picking* the string again. The secret is to hammer with the very tip of your finger, not the soft pad. Allow the second note to ring.

Example 5a

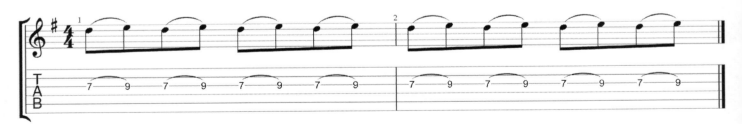

The following line combines a picked note with two hammer-ons. Only pick the first note and hammer onto the 5th and 7th fret with your second and fourth fingers respectively.

Example 5b

You can hammer on from an open string to a fretted note.

Example 5c

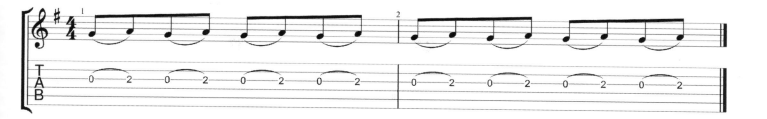

Pull-offs

It's probably no surprise, but a pull-off is the exact opposite of a hammer-on. You pick a note and pull your finger off to sound a lower pitched note.

A pull-off is again shown by a curved line over a note and looks identical to that of a hammer-on. Sometimes you'll see the letters "P/O" over the notes, but if that's not there, you must look at the pitches themselves to see whether the music calls for a hammer-on or pull off.

If the pitch of the notes ascends, use a hammer-on.

If the pitch of the notes descends, use a pull-off.

In the following example, place your third finger on the 9th fret of the third string, and *also* place your first finger on the 7th fret of the same string.

Pick the 9th fret note and pull the third finger off (down, towards the floor) to sound the note on the 7th fret without picking the string again.

Your third finger should act as a "mini pick" on your fretting hand and you need to be careful not to catch the second string as you pull-off towards the floor.

Let the note on the 7th fret ring out cleanly.

Example 5d

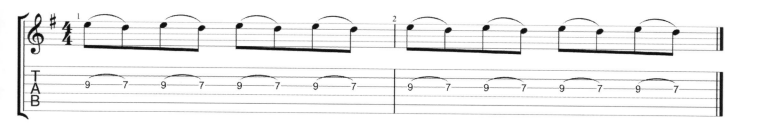

Hammer-ons and pull-offs can be played over any reachable distance. In the next example, use your fourth finger to play the higher note and pull off to your first finger to play the lower note.

Example 5e

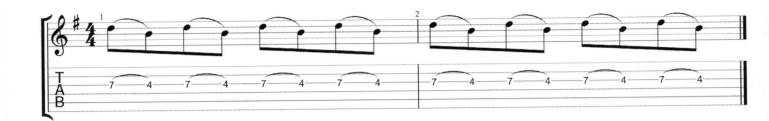

It's also possible to pull off to an open string. Stevie Ray Vaughan used this technique a lot in his fast-paced blues.

Example 5f

Hammer-ons and pull-offs are often combined into long sequences and the only time you pick the guitar is on the first note or when changing strings. All the other notes can be played legato.

In this example, I've written a slightly longer phrase the combines hammer-ons, pull-offs and the occasional picked note which is marked with the picking directions you learned in the previous chapter.

Remember, ascending notes are hammer-ons and descending notes are pull-offs.

Example 5g

One final combination of hammer-ons and pull-offs that you're likely to encounter in modern music is the trill. A trill is a rapid hammer-on and pull-off between two notes.

Trills are marked with a "tr" above the note in question, and will feature the note your trilling from, and the note you're trilling to, in brackets. In the following example, at the end of the first bar, pick the open G string, then trill to the 2nd fret.

Example 5h

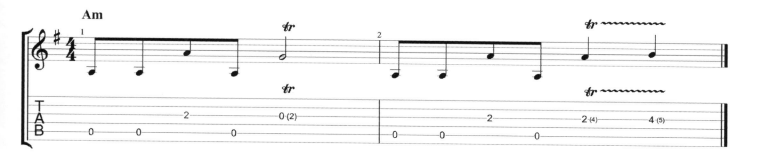

Right-Hand Tapping

The first recorded example of a guitarist tapping a note on the guitar was in 1965 by the Italian, Vittorio Camardese, but the technique was popularised by Eddie Van Halen, Stanley Jordan and Steve Hackett in the 1970s and '80s.

Tapping is quite an advanced legato technique where a picking-hand finger reaches across and "taps" a note on the fretboard of the guitar. The word *tap* is a bit misleading in my opinion – the movement is more like a hammer-on and immediate pull-off with a picking-hand finger.

When combined with left-hand hammer-ons and pull-offs, tapping allows guitarists to play extremely fast phrases without the need for a pick.

To perform a tap, begin by holding down the 5th fret on the second string and pick the string normally with the pick. Next, use the middle finger of the right hand to tap firmly down onto the 12th fret of the same string and smoothly "pluck" the string with the right-hand finger by performing a pull-off down towards the floor. As you pull-off from the 12th fret with the finger of the right hand, the held 5th fret note should sound as if you've re-picked the string.

Keep holding the 5th fret down and repeatedly tap (hammer-on) and release (pull-off) the 12th fret note with the middle finger of the right hand.

In notation, the symbol for a tapped note is normally just a simple "T" above the tapped note.

Example 5i

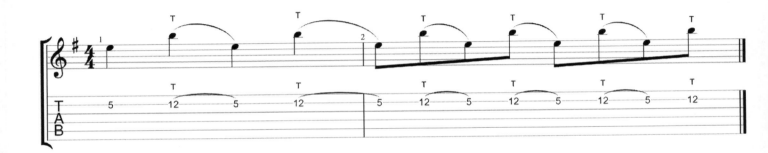

The next example combines hammer-ons and pull-offs in the left hand with a tapped note in the right hand. Only pick the first note in the sequence once. After the initial pick, you should be able to keep the notes sounding by using hammer-ons and pull-offs. Pay attention to the legato markings in the tab.

Example 5j

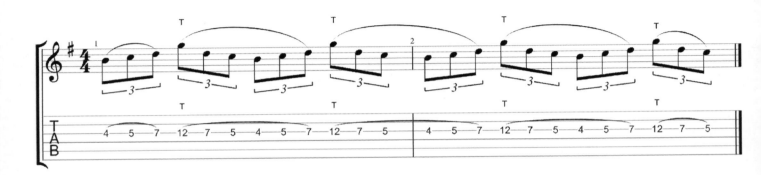

The next example begins with a tap and descends through the previous sequence.

Example 5k

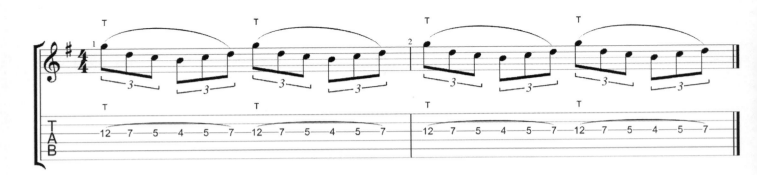

When tapping, it's often possible to omit the picking completely by using a *hammer-on from nothing*. Quite simply this is the technique of hammering on the first note in a phrase and it's like performing a tap with the left hand. You must develop some left-hand strength to manage this, but it's a worthwhile technique to learn.

The symbol for a hammer-on-from-nothing is similar to the symbol for a normal hammer-on, it just doesn't have a starting note. This is a tricky technique, so don't worry if you don't get it immediately.

In the following example, tap the 4th fret firmly with the index finger of your fretting hand and play through the sequence of notes adding the tap on the 12th fret with the middle finger of the picking hand.

Example 5l

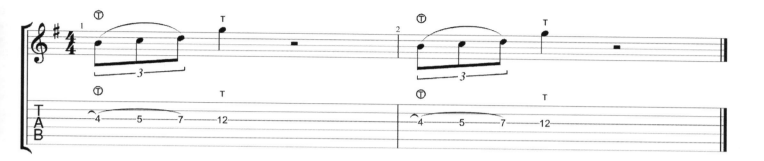

Finally, one other tapping technique you may come across is the *tap and slide*. This is where the finger of the picking hand taps a note, then slides the tapped note up or down to another pitch before releasing the tap. The notation for a tap and slide is as you might expect: a T over the tapped notes and a diagonal slide line to show the movement of the note.

In the following example, fret and pick the first note normally and hammer on to the 7th fret and hold it. Next, hammer on to the 12th fret with the middle finger of the right hand. Keep the pressure on with the right-hand tap and slide the tapped note up to the 14th fret and back down to the 12th. The tapped note should change pitch smoothly and ring throughout the movement. When the tapped note returns to the 12th fret, pull off with the right-hand finger to sound the 7th fret again before pulling off to 5th fret.

Example 5m

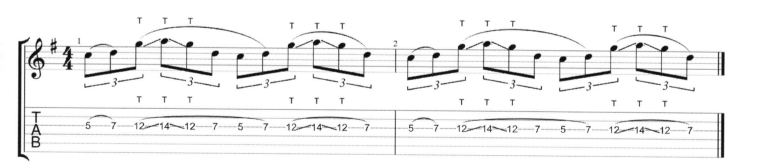

Tapping is a great technique and often guitarists will cheekily use the time where the tapped note is being played to quickly change position with the left hand, leading to some pretty far-out sounding licks.

Fundamental Changes will soon be publishing a dedicated book on tapping, so watch this space!

Chapter Six: Articulation and Dynamics

Often, music calls for you to *articulate* individual notes in specific ways. Other times, a whole passage or phrase should be played louder, softer, or gradually moving from one volume to another.

The catch-all term for these techniques is *dynamics* and in this chapter I'll show you what you can expect to see written on a piece of guitar tab.

Articulation

When playing rock, funk, pop or metal, the number one most common articulation you'll see is the palm mute. This is performed by lightly resting the fleshy "heel" of the picking hand slightly on the strings, right by the bridge of the guitar. Most of your hand will be in contact with the bridge, and a small portion should be touching the strings. The more of your hand that touches the strings, the bigger the mute will be.

A palm muted passage is shown in tab by the letters P.M. above or below the notes and small dots or hyphens under the passage that should be muted.

I've shown how palm muting is notated below. In bar one, allow the first two beats to ring out and mute the second two. In bar two, let the melody ring for two beats and mute it for two beats.

Example 6a

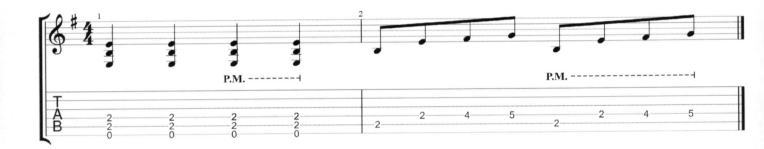

The opposite of a palm mute might be considered the "let ring" indication. As the name suggests, when a passage is marked to "let ring", all notes should be held and ring into each other as much as possible.

The following example features a simple phrase played once without any marking, and then again ringing out.

Example 6b

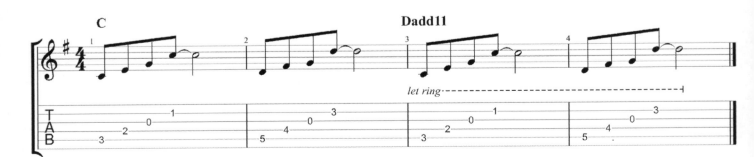

Another important articulation is simply called an *accent* and is shown by a ">" mark placed over a note. This symbol simply tells you to play that note slightly louder than all the others. In the following example, the third note in each bar is accented.

Example 6c

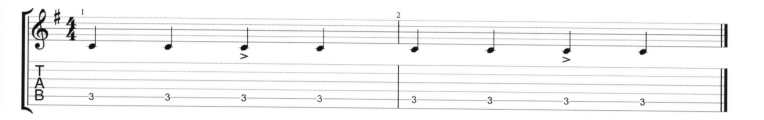

Be careful when playing an accent. It's easy to accidently make the accented note a bit shorter than the others around it as you dig in with your pick. Even though the note is louder, it still lasts for the same duration as all the others.

However, if you *do* want to make a note short and detached, the technique you're looking for is *staccato*. Staccato is Italian for "sharply detached and separated from the others" and is shown in music by a single dot directly over or under the note.

To play a staccato note, you can play it as normal, then quickly reduce pressure on the string with your fretting finger, or quickly palm mute after the initial pick strike with your right hand.

In the following example, the third note in each bar is played staccato. It's tough not to add a bit of an accent to the note when you're playing staccato, but try to avoid doing so.

Example 6d

One articulation you will rarely see in tablature is the *marcato* which is essentially an accented staccato note. It is shown by a **v** above the note.

In the following example, the third note in each bar is played as a marcato. Play it as a short, detached and accented note.

Example 6e

One final articulation marking to consider is the "fermata". This affects the timing of a phrase and indicates you should hold the note before continuing. When playing solo, the length of the note is at the player's discretion. In a band setting, you'll need to follow whoever is leading the band.

The example below features four bars of music with a *fermata* at the end of the second bar. It's placed here to help the music breathe.

Example 6f

Dynamics

While articulations are techniques that are applied to single notes, *dynamics* generally refer to volume changes that effect whole musical phrases.

As with many things in music, the words and markings that describe loud and quiet come from the original Italian language. *Piano* (pronounced Pee-ah-no) means quiet, and *forte* (pronounced fort-eh[1]) means loud.

Piano is abbreviated to "p" and forte is abbreviated to "f".

The more P's, the quieter you play, and the more F's the louder you play.

So "p" means play quietly, "pp" means play very quietly, and "ppp" is barely audible. (Incidentally, *pp* stands for *pianissimo*, which means "play very quietly" in Italian!)

Conversely, "f" means play loudly, "ff" means play very loudly, and "fff" means, well… go nuts! (*ff* stands for *fortissimo*, which is Italian for "play very loudly").

---

1. Possibly where a Canadian army lives.

As guitarists, it's worth mentioning that when you see *fff* written above the music, this doesn't mean turn your amplifier up, it means play harder!

There's another Italian term you should know: *mezzo*. This means medium, or middle. You will often see dynamics like *mp* (fairly quiet) and *mf* (fairly loud). If you put me on the spot, I'd say that most music without any dynamic markings would normally be played as *mf* (mezzo forte).

In the example below, the first bar is played *p*, the second bar is played *mf*, the third bar is played *f*, and the final bar is played *fff*.

Example 6g

Dynamics don't always jump dramatically, as in the previous example. Often they move gradually between two different volumes. For example, a passage might move slowly from quiet to loud, or loud to quiet over a period of four or eight bars. To show this we use the signs < (*crescendo* / get louder) and > (*diminuendo* get quieter).

Normally, the start and end volumes will be given. For example, *ppp* < *fff* means start very quietly and get louder. Sometimes this will happen over a period of just a few beats, which signifies a very dramatic change.

In the following example I move from *pp* to *ff* over a period of four bars. Notice how the crescendo sign is stretched between the volume markings.

Example 6h

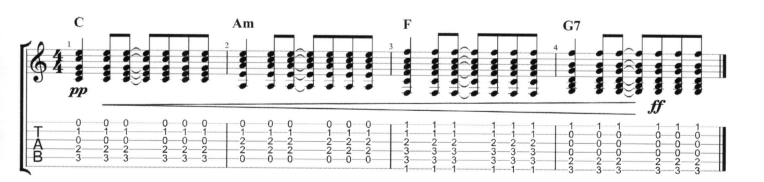

And here's the same thing with a diminuendo from *ff* to *pp*.

Example 6i

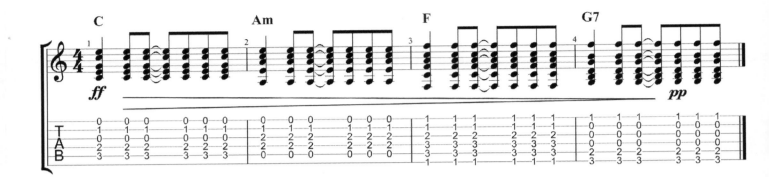

You may also see smaller changes in volume localised to single notes on electric guitar. These are indicated with small hairpins on each note and are executed by playing the note with the volume off, then rolling it on. This effect removes the attack of the note and creates a violin-like sound.

Example 6j

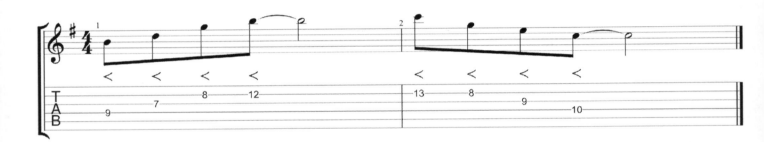

There was quite a lot of information in this section, which I summarise in the table below, but the crux of it is *p* = quiet, *f* = loud, < = get louder and > = get quieter.

Dynamics and articulation are often overlooked in music, but they're one of the most important factors in making your music sound expressive and emotional.

pp (pianissimo)	Very quiet
p (piano)	Quiet
mp (mezzo piano)	Quite quiet
mf (mezzo forte)	Quite loud
f (forte)	Loud
ff (fortissimo)	Very loud
< (crescendo)	Get louder
> (Diminuendo)	Get quieter

Chapter Seven: Harmonics

It's a little outside the remit of this book, but the way harmonics work is actually quite interesting. It's all about creating a *node* on the string so that it vibrates in two separate sections.

The simplest harmonic to play is the *natural harmonic*. To create one, touch the string *very* gently over the 12th fret (don't push the string down to the fret) and pick the string. As you pick the string, gently lift your finger off the string. The 12th fret is precisely in the middle of the string, and if you have done it right, the point where you were touching the string will be completely still, while the two lengths of string either side of that point will resonate equally.

The note you have created is one octave higher in pitch than the open string.

To show a natural harmonic, the fretted note is surrounded by the symbols < >, and in the notation part you'll see a diamond note head.

Example 7a

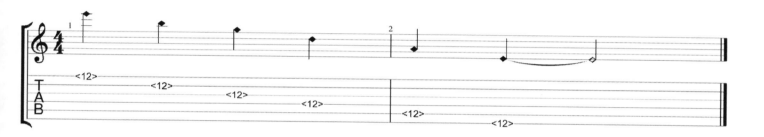

Natural harmonics can be created at any point on the guitar, where you can divide the string into an even ratio – for example, 2:1 (as above) 3:1, or 4:1.

This means that you can play natural harmonics on frets 12, 7, 5, 4, and even 3.2. As you descend the neck, the harmonics get harder to play as you need to be more precise on a smaller target. If you're struggling, try adding a little distortion to help.

Example 7b

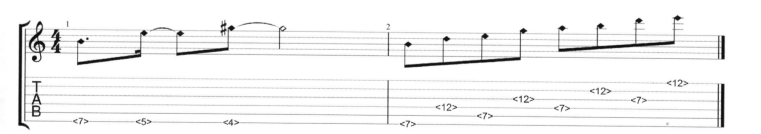

Pinched harmonics (*squealies*) work on a similar principle to natural harmonics, but in this case the note is created by the picking hand as you play a note with your fretting hand.

The technique is a little hard to describe in words. In essence, you need to contact the string with the pick and, as you follow through, immediately touch a node (a location on the string where harmonics can occur) on the same string with the edge of your thumb. This is performed as a single action. Use some distortion and add a bit of vibrato to the fretted note to help the pinched harmonic ring out.

As with natural harmonics, the node points are in ratios of the string length, but as you can create a pinched harmonic on any fretted note, the locations move around.

To get started, hold down the 7th fret of the 3rd string and position your picking hand around the area of the middle pickup (on a Stratocaster-type guitar). Pick the 3rd string downwards, fairly hard, touching the string with the side of your thumb as you follow through.

If the pinched harmonic doesn't ring out, it will be because you are not quite on a node. Move your picking hand a small amount in either direction until you find the sweet spot that will cause the harmonic to ring out. Don't forget to add some vibrato and use some distortion on your amp.

When you hit the right spot, you'll hear the pinched harmonic sound an octave above the fretted note. The notation for a pinched harmonic is like that of a natural harmonic, however you'll notice the letters P.H. or A.H. above the note, and the location of the right-hand pick in a tiny <> bracket next to it.

Example 7c

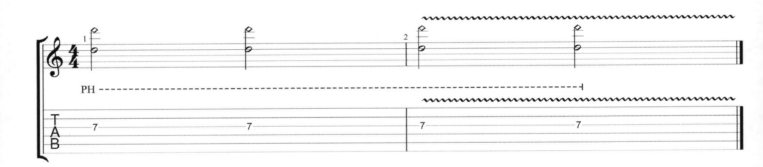

Sometimes you'll see a pinched harmonic written inside a diamond or a triangle, and the exact pitch of the harmonic written in below. Locating the pitch of the harmonic is often a matter of trial and error, and is achieved by moving the position where you strike the guitar.

When you've nailed the technique above, experiment with the location where you pick the string. As you move forward and back from the bridge to the neck, you'll find different pitches of harmonics, just as you did with the natural harmonics earlier.

Example 7d

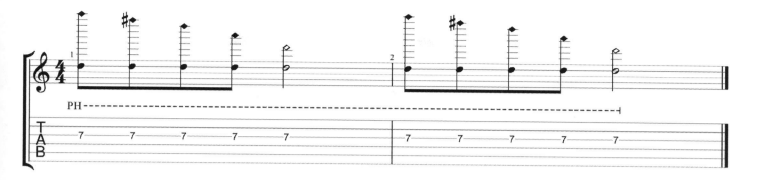

Pinched harmonics are used all the time in rock guitar soloing and often done indiscriminately. They're a great way to suddenly introduce a very high pitched note into a solo. Check out this short solo example.

Example 7e

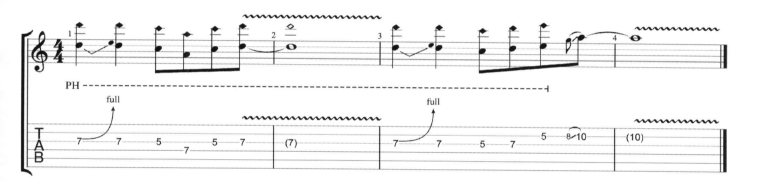

Tapped harmonics are closely related to natural harmonics, but involve *tapping* a note a set distance above a fretted note. They're normally notated in the same way as a natural harmonic, with the letters T.H. written over the top.

The easiest way to get started is to fret a note low down on the guitar and tap 12 frets above the note directly onto the fret bar. In the example below, hold down the second fret and tap directly onto the wire of the 14th fret. Tap hard and quickly. Bounce off, so that your finger is in contact with the string for the shortest possible time.

Example 7f

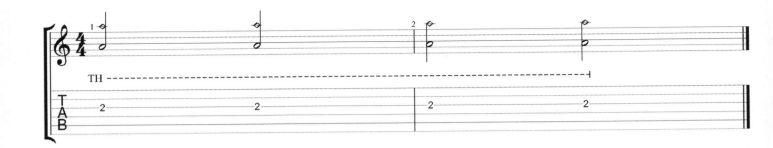

Again, as with many things in life, it's all about that ratio! You can create harmonics by tapping 12, 7, 5, and 4 etc, frets above the fretted note. It's useful to think of the tap on the 12th fret above as zero, so you can move these ratios both up and down the string.

In the following example, I hold the 2nd fret down and tap the fret wire of the various harmonic points on the 3rd string. Add a little vibrato in your fretting hand to make the harmonics ring.

Example 7g

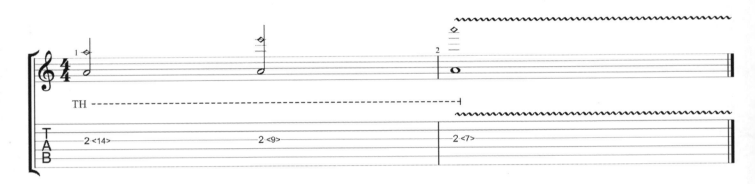

One beautiful application of tapped (and indeed harp harmonics which we'll cover in a minute) is to hold down a chord in your fretting hand, and tap 12 frets above the chord with your right hand. If you use your middle finger you can continue to hold your pick normally. Remember to tap hard, fast and directly onto the fret wire.

Example 7h

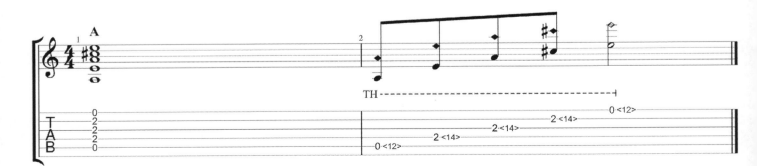

52

Finally, *artificial* and *harp harmonics* are tricky little beasts that, in fairness, sound incredible. In essence, this technique involves holding down a fretted note (or more typically a chord) and picking a harmonic 12 frets above that note (or notes).

In order to sound the harmonic, hold down a note with your fretting hand (for example, an A note on the third string, 2nd fret). Now position your picking hand index finger over the fret wire of the 14th fret. Touch the string lightly above the 14th fret, pick the string with a spare finger or thumb, and immediately lift off your index finger.

The spare digit used to pluck the string will vary from player to player, depending on what you find most comfortable. I tuck my thumb behind my index finger and point at the fret, then pluck the string with my thumb. Other players do it the classical way and pluck with their ring finger. Others, who prefer to use a plectrum, switch to holding the pick with the thumb and middle finger. Whether you use your thumb, finger, or a pick, make sure to tuck in behind the index finger, as this will help when it comes to harp harmonics.

Example 7i

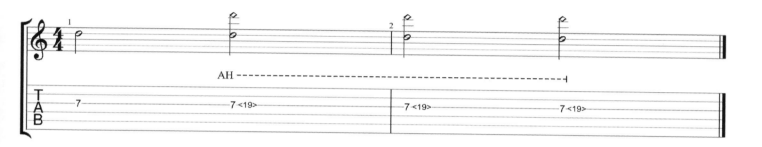

Harp harmonics is a technique achieved by combining artificial harmonics with regular picked strings. The "harp" effect is created by plucking an artificial harmonic, followed by a fretted note, followed by another artificial harmonic, and so on. The notes are allowed to ring into each other and should sound for as long as possible.

To play a harp harmonic:

• Hold down a chord

• Play the first note as an artificial harmonic, plucking 12 frets above, using the technique described above

• Play the next note in the chord as a normal fretted note (some players skip to the third note instead, to create a wider interval)

• Play the next note as an artificial harmonic

• Repeat until you have played through the whole chord

The combination of harmonic and normal fretted notes should create a "cascading" effect, also referred to as a *harmonic roll*. Use the index finger and thumb to play the harmonics and the ring finger to pluck the notes.

Example 7j

Harmonics are a beautiful playing technique, but their notation is one of the least standardised in modern guitar music. Often it's easy to tell what's required from the context, so look out for the letters "P.H.", "T.H." or "H.H." to give you a clue.

Chapter Eight: Whammy Bar Techniques

There are various makes and designs of *whammy bars* (sometimes erroneously named *tremolo bars*) available, and they all function in slightly different ways. However, the purpose of them all is to mechanically raise or lower the pitch of a note on the guitar.

When you press down on the whammy bar, the tension on the strings slackens, and any note that is sounding lowers in pitch, sometimes dramatically depending on how far you push it! Attached to the back of the bridge, and hidden inside the guitar, are a set of springs that return the whammy bar to its neutral position when the pressure is released.

Some whammy bars can be set so that not only can you depress the bar to lower the pitch of the note(s), you can pull back on it to raise them too.

Whammy bars have been around for about 70 years, and were invented by the luthier Paul Bigsby. However, they really came into their own in the late 1960s with Jimmy Hendrix's protest rendition of *The Star Spangled Banner*. Jeff Beck has been a great exponent of the whammy bar throughout his career, with his astonishing *'Cause We've Ended as Lovers* being an iconic example of his skill.

In the '80s and '90s, the whammy bar found new prominence amongst players such as Eddie Van Halen, Adrian Belew, Joe Satriani and Steve Vai, all of whom pushed the boundaries of the instrument using the cutting edge Floyd Rose systems of the day.

When notating the use of the whammy bar, the shape of the note manipulation is drawn onto the tablature over the affected notes. These lines sync up rhythmically with the notes below.

The first technique is to add some simple vibrato to a note using the bar. Pick a note as normal and repeatedly press the bar quickly and shallowly to create a smooth vibrato. As you see, the tablature for this technique is a more angled vibrato line that is sharper than the lines we use for standard vibrato. Sometimes you'll see the words "w/bar" added to a normal vibrato line.

Example 8a

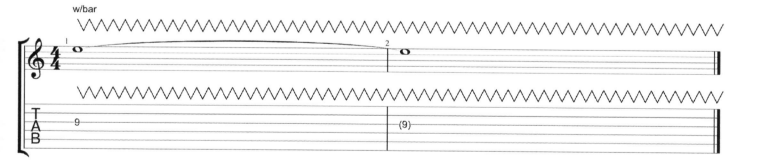

The next most common technique is to move (usually descend) from one defined pitch to another. In the first bar of the next example, the note E is held for one beat then lowered via the bar by one tone. As you can see, the whammy bar movement is notated above the tab and includes the contour of the movement and the distance the note should be lowered.

In the next bar, I lower the note by a semitone and in bar three I lower the note by 1.5 tones.

Example 8b

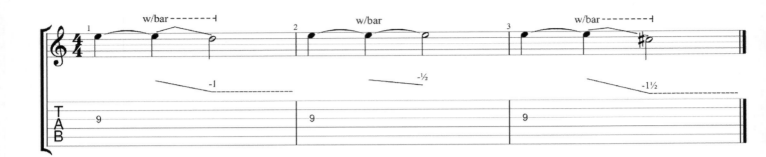

Of course, once depressed, the bar needs to return to pitch, and if this is to be audible it needs to be shown in the notation. It may not surprise you to know that the sign for this is a diagonal line pointing in the opposite direction.

Example 8c

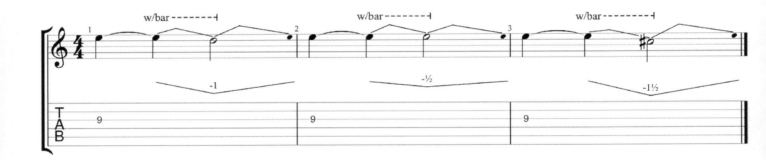

When reading tab, you may need to pay attention to the exact point and speed at which the whammy bar is pressed, how long it's dipped for, and how long it takes to return to pitch. While the following examples all look similar and lower the note by one tone, they all have different phrasing. Listen to the audio to hear how each of the following four whammy bar uses sound.

Example 8d

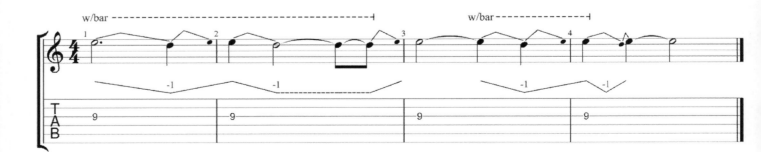

Another common whammy bar technique is the *dip*. This is really not much more than a fast, controlled push down on the bar that quickly lowers the note and immediately uses the springs to return it to pitch. Again, the symbol for this is fairly straightforward, but pay attention to when the dip occurs in the following two examples.

Example 8e

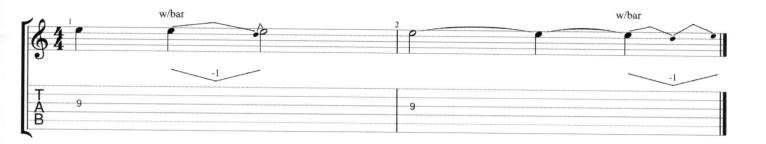

A whammy bar *scoop* is the technique of slightly pressing the bar (about 1/4 to half a tone), picking the desired pitch, and releasing the whammy bar to quickly bring the intended note into tune from below. It's a tricky little technique and a big part of Jeff Beck's guitar sound. A scoop is notated by a descriptively-shaped line that looks like a pre-bend. The following phrase uses scoops that begin from the scale step below the target note.

Example 8f

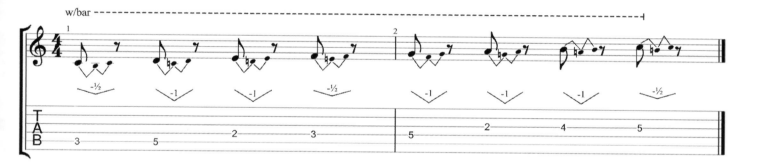

By pushing the whammy bar further you can create a *dive*. This sounds great on a single note or double stop, but for an awesome '80s vibe, try it with a 5th fret natural harmonic or high pitched pinched harmonic. Be careful to keep all the unused strings quiet.

Example 8g

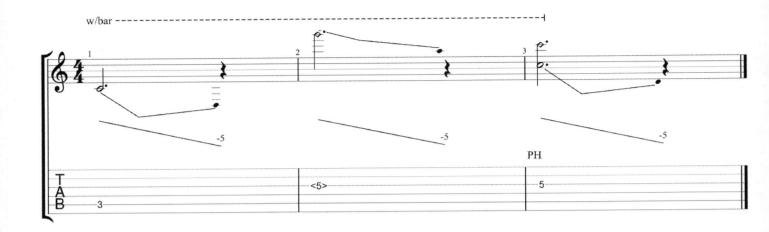

Finally, a technique that's only really possible on a floating or Floyd Rose system is the *flutter* or *gurgle*.

To play a flutter, point the whammy bar backwards towards the strap button of the guitar and aggressively flick it backwards to sound the note through the vibration of the tremolo. Again, there are various ways to notate this, but this is the most common symbol I've seen.

Example 8h

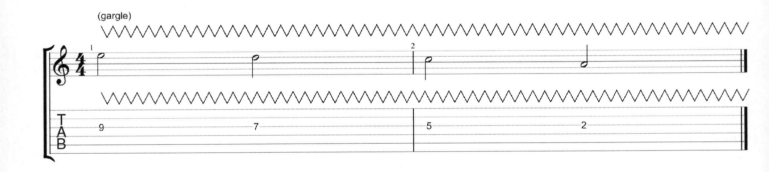

Chapter Nine: Structural Directions

In Chapter One, we covered some of the basics of the tablature score. We saw that there are six lines, one for each string, that music is divided into bars (measures) and beats. In this section we'll take a look at some of the other markings on the page that show us in which order to play the music.

Bar Lines

There are a few different types of bar lines you'll come across when reading guitar tablature. The first is simply a straight line that divides the music and makes it easier to read. Here's a short melody that's divided into four bars.

Example 9a

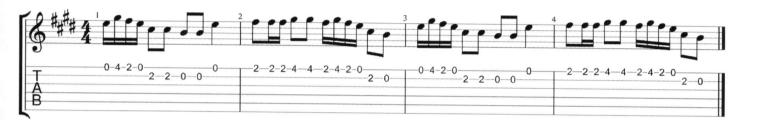

When you played through Example 9a you probably noticed that the melody was played twice. Musicians are naturally lazy, so we've come up with some special bar lines that tell the performer to repeat everything between them. A double bar line with two vertical dots is a *repeat* symbol. A repeated phrase will be sandwiched between two repeat bars. Notice that the dots are on the side of the lines that contain the repeat.

Example 9b sounds identical to Example 9a:

Example 9b

A double bar line shows that one section of the music has ended and another is beginning.

Example 9c

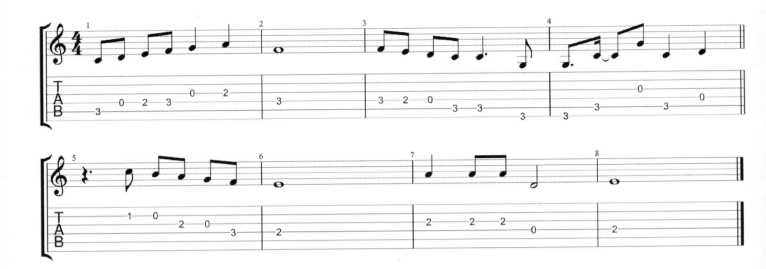

Simile marks function in a similar way to repeat marks, but are generally reserved for chordal or riff-based sections. Drummers use them a lot as their parts are normally quite repetitive.

A simile mark looks like a % sign and, when placed in an empty bar, means *repeat the previous bar*. In the following example, you would play the first bar then repeat it four times.

Example 9d

Simile marks can also be placed between two bars and written directly onto the bar line to show that any number of previous bars should be repeated. The number of lines in the simile sign tells you how many bars to repeat.

For example, in the notation below, the simile sign tells you to repeat the previous two bars.

Example 9e

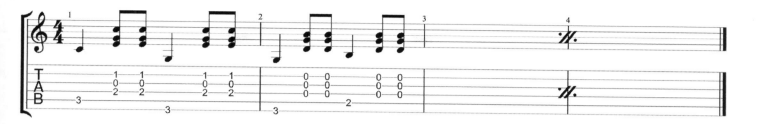

Volta brackets used to confuse the heck out of me as a child, but actually they're quite simple. You can think of them as different endings to play after a repeated section.

In the following example, play the eight-bar chord progression and repeat it according to the repeat marks. On the second time through, instead of playing the final bar under the 1st-time ending, play the bar under the 2nd-time ending.

Example 9f

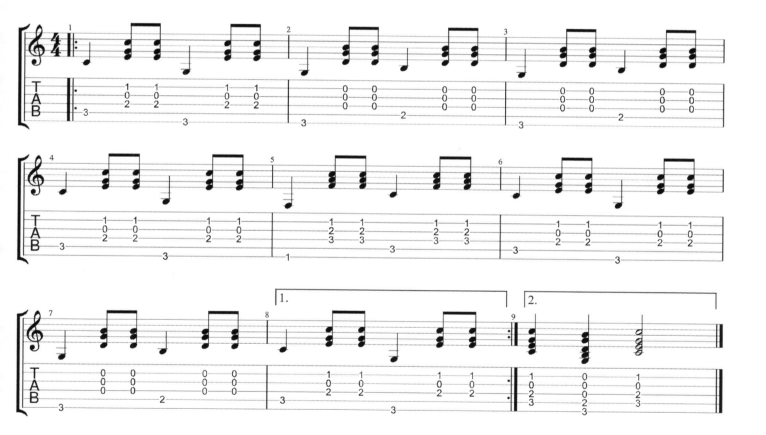

NB: It's possible to have more than two endings, you can have a 1st-time, 2nd-time and 3rd-time ending etc.

A piece of text you may come across occasionally is *Da Capo* (or *D.C.*). This is Italian and means "from the beginning". It's normally found right at the end of a piece and tells you to repeat the whole piece of music.

The word *fine*, (Italian for "end") is often placed earlier in the music and shows where you should finish the piece after taking the Da Capo. Often you will see the phrase *Da Capo al fine* (or *D.C. al fine*), which means "go back to the start of the piece and keep playing until you see the word *Fine*."

In Example 9g, play the four-bar phrase until the *D.C. al fine* marking, then start again from the beginning and end on the word *Fine* in bar three.

Example 9g

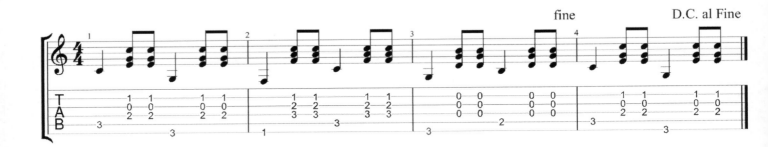

Sometimes the music doesn't require you to go all the way back to the beginning of the piece. Instead, you may need to go back to a specific bar or section. The way to notate this is with a *Dal Segno* or *D.S.* (pronounced *sen-yo*). The Segno is a little sign that looks like an S with a / through it and could appear at any point in the music.

D.S. al fine means "go back to the segno sign and play to the end. While the following example is quite short, imagine how much time this system would have saved a few hundred years ago when writing symphonies for 100 instruments with a quill.

In the next example, play the four-bar phrase and take the *D.S. al fine*. The segno is at the beginning of bar three, so you will play six bars in total. Listen to the audio if you're not sure what to do.

Example 9h

A final instruction you may come across is *Da Capo al coda* (D.C al coda) or *Dal Segno al coda* (D.S. al Coda)

A coda is shown by the symbol ⊕ and is (normally) a short section added onto the end of a piece of music to bring it to a satisfying conclusion. In modern music they're normally between four to sixteen bars long and could be a "repeat till fade" vamp, or any other myriad ways of ending a song.

So when you see the phrase *Da Capo al coda* (or *D.C. al coda*), it means "go back to the beginning, play through until you see the word *da coda* (or the sign ⊕), then jump to the coda section that's written after the main body of the music."

The phase *Da Segno al coda* (or *D.S. al coda*), means "go back to the segno sign, play through until you see the word *da coda* (or the sign ⊕), then jump to the coda section that's written after the main body of the music."

In Example 9i, I've used *D.C al coda*, so play through the whole four bars, go back to the beginning and play until the coda sign at the end of bar two. Jump forward to the coda section at the end of the music (also shown by the coda mark) and repeat it as shown by the repeat marks. End on the third bar of the coda after playing the repeated section.

Example 9i

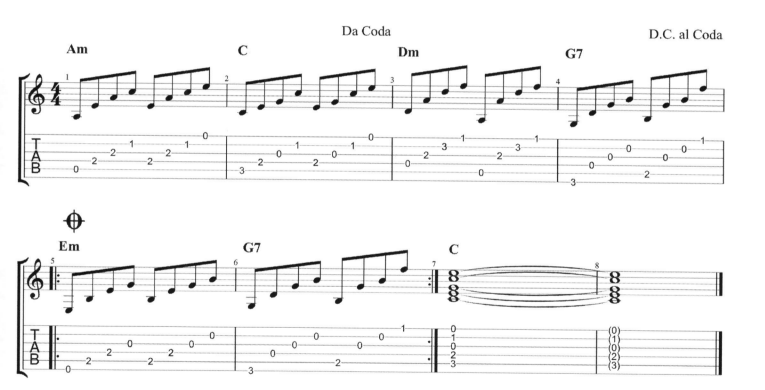

When you're getting started, D.C. markings can be a little confusing and you definitely have to keep your eyes out for them. However, once you know how they work you can save yourself a great deal of writing and quickly jot down ideas to give to your band mates. Recognising them in tab is an essential skill.

Conclusion

Well, we made it! What started off as me wanting to write a quick reference guide for my students has become a bit of a monster – but I hope it has equipped you to read the many and varied nuances of guitar technique you'll come across in music. A great next step would be to dig out some transcripts of your favourite solos and examine the tab to spot the things we've discussed here. Why not try composing a solo of your own, then tab it out, using the articulation and dynamics markings taught in this book?

Next, it's time to move on to master all the chords and rhythms you'll ever need on guitar. Check out The First 100 Chords for Guitar – coming up next!

Guitar: The First 100 Chords for Guitar

How to Learn and Play Guitar Chords: The Complete Beginner Guitar Method

Published by **www.fundamental-changes.com**

Copyright © 2019 Joseph Alexander

The moral right of this author has been asserted.

www.fundamental-changes.com

Twitter: **@guitar_joseph**

Over 10,000 fans on Facebook: **FundamentalChangesInGuitar**

Instagram: **FundamentalChanges**

For over 350 Free Guitar Lessons with Videos Check Out

www.fundamental-changes.com

Introduction

The first chords you learn on guitar may take you some time. Not only are you learning to use your fingers in a completely new way, you also have to learn some intricate muscle movements and commit those to subconscious memory. If you're a musician, or have ever played a sport, you may have heard the term 'muscle memory'.

Muscle memory is the name for something that is so automated we no longer have to think about it. Walking, riding a bike, throwing a ball and swimming are all examples of processes where we need to develop muscle memory to do them well. They are *learned* processes which may have taken some time to develop (probably since you were very young), but once you know them, the movements go to a very deep part of your brain and you don't need to actively think about them to make them work.

In fact, if you tried to think about the exact sequence of muscles you need to trigger in order to walk, then you would never get anywhere at all!

Walking probably took you a good few months to figure out, but now you probably never think about having to do it at all. Remember this fact while you're taking your first steps on guitar. For many people, playing chords isn't an instant skill and it will take a while before their precise movements are committed to muscle memory. To put chords firmly into muscle memory we need to do a bit of structured (yet fun!) practice, where we train our brains exactly how to form each chord, and how to move from one chord to another.

Chords need to be locked into our muscle memory because we don't have a lot of time to form, or change between them when playing songs. If we change too slowly there will be a big hole in the rhythm and flow of the song. To use a sporting analogy again: imagine what would happen if you had to actually think about blocking every time someone threw a punch in a boxing match. We need to build chords to the point where they become a reflex reaction.

Developing this skill isn't as hard as it may seem… it just takes a bit of commitment, regular practice and a structured approach to learning. As adults, we sometimes don't like to learn new things. It's easy to feel that learning finished when we left school or college, so we can sometimes shy away from new challenges or experiences. Music, however, is a really fun habit to get into. The results can be quick and effortless, or sometimes slow and challenging. Either way, the end result – playing music – is one of the most rewarding experiences you can have.

If you want to use this book as a reference, you can dive straight in now. However, in the final chapters I have included some really useful tips on how to practice efficiently, develop some great playing habits that will stay with you for life, and move from learning chords to playing songs by adding rhythm. These sections will teach you to learn and memorise chords more quickly, turn you into a better musician, and help you develop a healthy approach to the guitar.

Two questions that guitar teachers get asked regularly are:

How long will it take to learn to play the guitar?

And,

How many chords are there?

Both are quite difficult to answer.

The first is difficult to answer because it has a lot of variables. For example, how much will you practice? Will you focus on the right things? *How* will you practice? How do you define 'being able to play the guitar'? Do you just want to strum a few chords around a campfire or is it your goal to become the next Eddie Van Halen?

With all these variables and more, it is almost impossible to give a straight answer or time frame. But, if you practice for about twenty minutes every day, practice efficiently and are aiming to play some chord-based pop music, then it normally takes a few months to get fairly competent.

In answer to the second question, the answer is simply 'lots, but as a guitarist you will probably use relatively few of them'. Luckily for us, once you've learned a few 'open' chords and a few 'barre' chords, you can play pretty much any chord or song on the guitar.

Let's get started and look at the *open position* chords available to us. If you're a beginner, I highly recommend working through Chapter One in conjunction with the How to Practice section at the end of the book.

A Final Note!

PLEASE download and listen to the audio along with each example. It will really help you develop as a player. It takes a lot longer to reach a goal if you don't know what that goal looks (or sounds) like.

Get the audio from **www.fundamental-changes.com**. It's free ☺

How to Read Chord Diagrams

The following images show how the written notation of a chord diagram relates to where you place your fingers on the neck of the guitar to play a chord. Pay careful attention to which strings are played and which fingers are use.

The first diagram shows the notes on each of the open strings of the guitar.

The second diagram shows you how to number the fingers of the fretting hand. If you are left-handed, the same numbers apply to your right hand

The third diagram shows the standard way chords are notated on chord *girds*. Each dot represents where you place a finger.

The final diagram shows how the notation relates to where you place your fingers on the guitar neck.

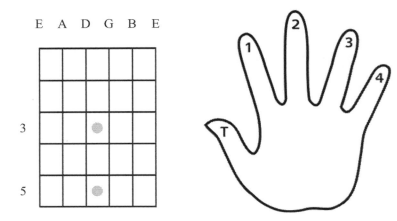

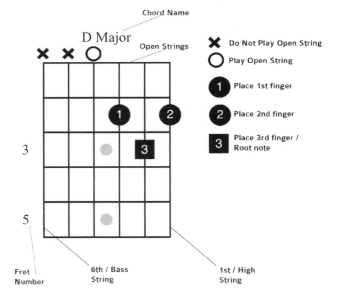

Chapter One: Open Position Chords

Open position chords are normally the first chords people learn on the guitar. They are named 'open position' chords because they often use open strings as notes within the chord. As you will see later, there are many chords which do not use open strings.

Open position chords can be used to play the majority of songs that you hear on the radio (depending on your taste in music!). They are great to use while songwriting because they are relatively easy to play, and provide a 'full-sounding' harmony to accompany vocals or other instruments.

Not all chords are easily accessible in the open position, but songs written by guitarists are normally in easy 'guitar keys', so you will find that the chords in this chapter cover most situations.

The first chord I teach my students is normally E Minor, or 'Em' for short. It looks like this as a chord diagram:

Example 1a:

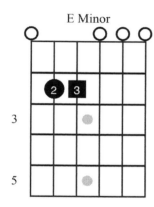

The root of the E Minor chord is the note 'E' and is played on the lowest open string (the thickest bass string). Look at how the above diagram relates to the neck image on the previous page.

Place your second finger on the 2nd fret of the 5th string, and then place your third finger on the 2nd fret of the 4th string, right next to it.

Make sure you use the correct fingers. It's tempting to use the first and second finger, but they will be needed a little later. Refer to the hand diagram on the previous page if you're not sure.

Now flick to the **How to Practice** section and work through the first set of exercises for learning new chords. Apply these steps to the Em chord.

Let's learn our second chord: A Minor, or Am.

Am is played like this.

Example 1b:

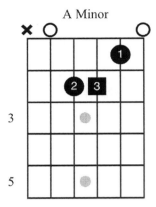

A Minor

Notice that there is an 'x' on the bottom string of the guitar, so do *not* play it. Strum the guitar from the 5th string downwards.

Compare the notes and fingering of Am to Em. Can you see that the second and third fingers both move across one string as a single unit and then the first finger is added on the second string?

Complete the steps in the **How to Practice** section and work with a metronome up to the target speed.

A quick note about your thumb

The thumb of the fretting hand should be placed on the back of the neck, roughly in line with the fingers but not necessarily directly behind them. This placement isn't a precise science, but the thumb provides support for the fretting fingers to squeeze against. Sometimes, the thumb may be closer to the head of the guitar than the fingers and it will normally find a slightly different position for each chord. As long as the hand is comfortable and each note rings clearly you should be fine.

Be aware though, if you're just starting out playing guitar, you'll probably have a tendency to 'over-squeeze' the neck when playing chords. Experiment with the smallest possible pressure you can use to play the chord cleanly. Fret the chord, and make sure that when you strum it, each note rings. Then simply relax the pressure gradually in your hand to find the minimum pressure needed to make the chord ring out.

When you feel confident playing both Em and Am separately, work through the steps in the **Learning Chords in Context section** of the **How to Practice** chapter, and learn how to combine the two chords together as a short piece of music.

Next, add some strumming to the chord progression using steps in Chapter Thirteen.

Listen for any buzzes and muted notes while you play each chord and try to minimise these as much as possible.

The next chord to learn is C Major. Notice that it has two fretted notes in common with Am. All you need to do to move from Am to C Major is move your third finger off the 3rd string, and on to the 3rd fret on the 5th string. This is a bit of a stretch at first, but adjust your thumb position on the back of the neck, and you will soon find a comfortable way to play the chord. Start your strum from the fifth string and avoid the sixth.

Example 1c:

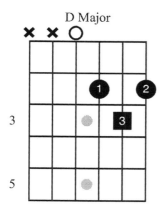

Compare the chords of Am and C Major to see how much they have in common. Use the steps in the **How to Practice** section learn the chord of C Major and then link it with the chord of Am.

The next chord to learn is D Major. Pay attention to the fingering and listen to the audio track so you can hear how it should sound.

Example 1d:

Learn D Major just as you learnt the previous three chords. First tackle it individually and build your muscle memory, then work through the steps to combine it with another chord. I recommend you combine it with Em to begin with.

G Major is a little harder because it uses all four fingers. Listen to the audio and practice matching the sound you hear. Be careful to pay attention to any buzzes or muted notes you create.

Example 1e:

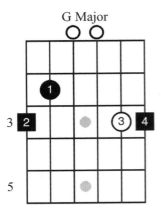

The white note is optional. If you decide not to play it, that's fine, but it's good to know it is an option.

Work through the steps to incorporate this chord into your vocabulary. I recommend that you pair G Major with Em for now. G Major is a challenging chord and Em is less difficult. If you really can't manage to play between G Major and Em in rhythm, simply strum on the open strings instead of the Em. It won't sound great, but it will help you build muscle memory on the G Major before adding the Em back into the sequence.

Our brains work best when learning new information in context, so practicing pairs of chords helps us learn the muscle memory of the chord change as well as the chord's sound, feel, and how it works in relation to other chords.

The following sets of chords are good to learn in pairs. Learn each one individually at first and then use the steps in the **How to Practice** section to build your muscle memory and fluency as you combine them. Some new chords are paired with chords you already know.

Example 1f:

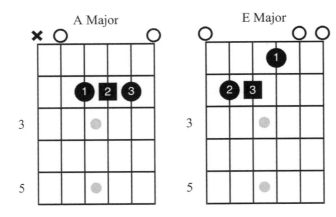

Example 1g:

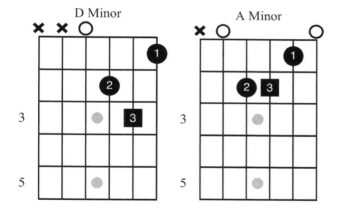

The next chord, F Major, is challenging as it uses a small *barre* to play two notes on the 1st fret. Getting a barre right is all about the position of your *thumb* (believe it or not!) Until now, your thumb has been placed towards the top of half of the neck and used to squeeze against the fretting fingers. With the F Major chord, experiment by allowing your thumb to drop right down to the bottom half of the guitar neck. This movement will rotate your wrist slightly and make it easier to get your first finger parallel to the fret wire to play the barre.

Learn F Major in conjunction with A Minor.

Example 1h:

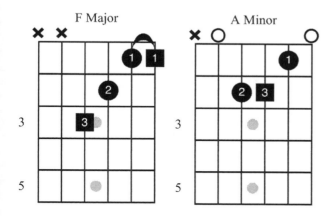

F Major is one of the more difficult chords, so if you are struggling it's okay to play the easier chord of F Major 7 (FMaj7). Instead of the barre, you can play the first string open.

Example 1i:

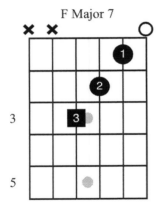

F Major 7

Test yourself and make some music!

After you have worked through the steps in the **How to Practice** section, try the following short chord progressions. You don't have to know all the chords in this chapter before you begin… just work with what you have. Add new chords as you learn them and get creative with your practice. Some chords sound better together than others, and trial and error is a great way to discover new and exciting sounds.

Example 1j:

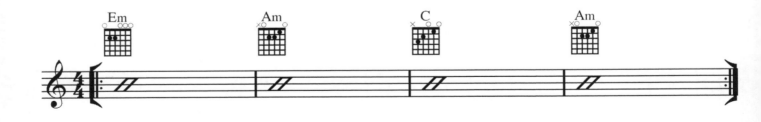

Example 1k:

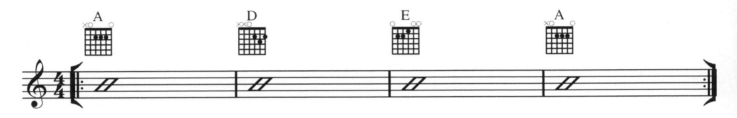

Example 1l:

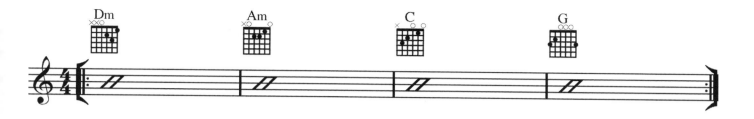

Example 1m:

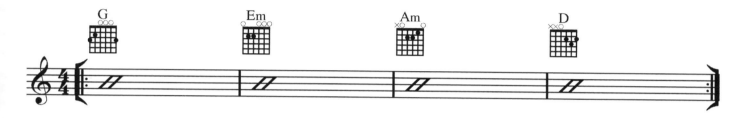

Example 1n:

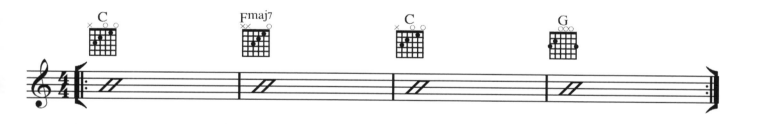

You'll probably begin by just strumming one chord per bar of music, but as you work further through the **How to Practice** section, start adding more rhythms and strumming patterns. There's a breakdown of how to strum rhythms on the guitar in **Chapter Thirteen**.

Think about *how* you play each chord… loud or soft? Gentle or Aggressive? Pick or no pick?

The most important thing is to listen carefully to what you play. Don't accept any muted notes or buzzes! Keep adjusting your fingers and thumb until each chord is clean. If you need to, go back to the muscle memory exercises on individual chords and make sure you are placing your fingers correctly

If your fingers get sore, take a break and come back later.

Have fun! You're making music.

Chapter Two: Dominant 7 Open Chords

The chords in this section are named *Dominant 7* chords. They have a slightly tense sound and often want to *resolve* that *tension* to another chord. These chords will expand your musical horizons and teach you some great new sounds.

As always, learn these chords in pairs. Combine a chord you don't know with one that you do, then practice moving between them. Each new chord is listed with a suggested friend you learnt in Chapter One.

Example 2a:

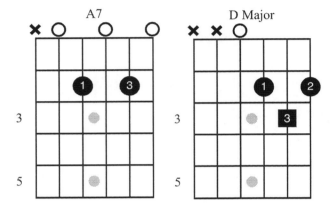

Example 2b:

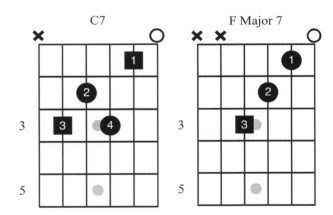

Example 2c:

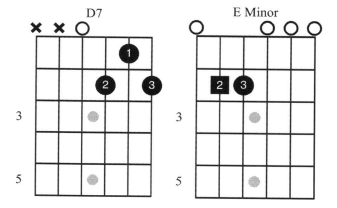

Example 2d:

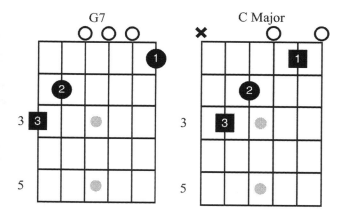

Example 2e: *On the B7, the second string can also be played open.*

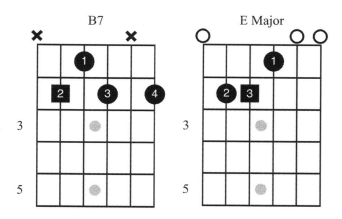

Example 2f:

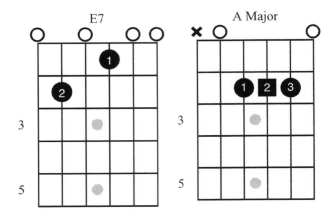

Test yourself!

Once you have introduced each new chord into your vocabulary by using the steps in the **How to Practice** section, work towards building the following short chord progressions. Begin by strumming one chord per bar and gradually add more interesting rhythms by working through **Chapter Thirteen.**

Example 2g:

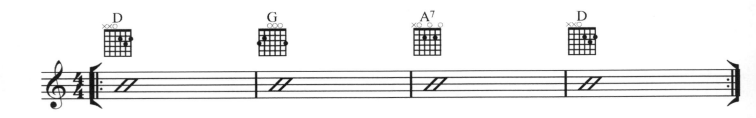

Example 2h:

Example 2i:

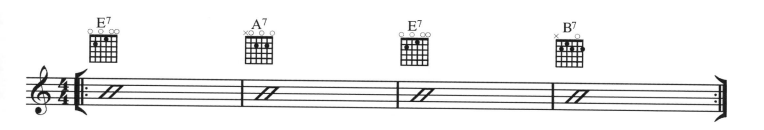

Example 2j:

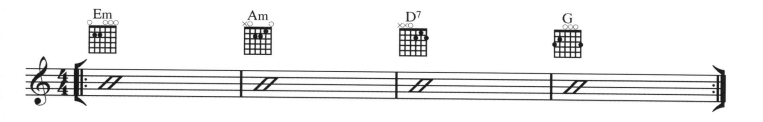

Example 2k:

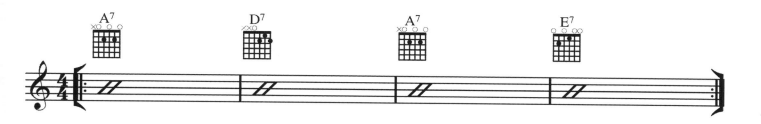

Chapter Three: Barre Chords

We will look at some more open chords in Chapter Five, but first it's time to learn some essential *barre* chords.

A barre chord uses a finger to make a bar (*barre* in Spanish, the birthplace of the guitar) across multiple strings. You saw a mini-barre in Chapter One in the chord of F Major. Now, however, we will learn to use a full-barre to form some new and important chord shapes.

Barre chords have an advantage over open chords: they're movable. It is possible to slide a barre chord up and down the strings to play different chords because barre chords don't contain any open strings.

For example, play an E Minor chord, then slide your fingers up one fret and strum the chord again. It sounds wrong because you moved some of the notes (the fretted ones) up the neck, but the notes on the open strings stayed put. If we could bring the open string with us when we move the chord up the neck, we could keep the relationship between all the notes the same and 'not leave any notes behind'.

Barre chords allow us to bring the open strings with us as we move chord shapes around the neck.

The first barre chord to learn is the 'minor' barre. Compare the barre chord version of Bm below, with the open position chord of Em.

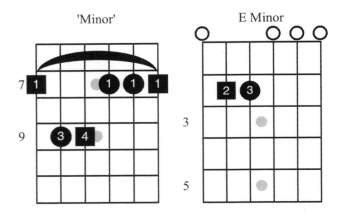

Can you see that these two chords are formed identically? The barre in the first diagram replaces the open strings in the second Em diagram.

The first chord hasn't been named, although when you place the barre at the 7th fret this just happens to be a Bm because the note at the 7th fret of the sixth string is B. We will look at this in more detail soon.

For now, practice forming the chord of Bm by placing your first finger across the strings at the 7th fret and using your third and fourth fingers to play the other notes.

Example 3a:

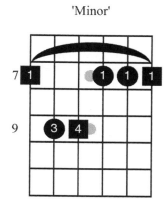

'Minor'

Playing a barre is tricky at first. Just as with the F Major chord in Chapter One, a big part of the secret is to move your thumb to the lower half of the neck. However, it is also important to place the barre finger on its *side* so that the nail of the finger *points towards the head of the guitar.*

If you place the finger so the nail points in the same direction as the fret wire, you will find that the strings fall into the little folds of your finger joints and become muted. By using the *bony side* of the finger, you will make a better contact with the strings and your chords will sound much cleaner.

Barre chords are always a challenge for beginners, but with a little perseverance and some analytic practice, you will get the knack of it in no time.

Work through the **How to Practice** steps to commit the barre chord to muscle memory. Don't worry if this takes a few days or weeks! Try combining it with an Em or a strum on open strings to help you master the movement.

The shape you have just learnt is a Minor barre chord with its root on the *sixth* string. Notice that the square root marker is on the lowest string of the guitar. The chord written above is a B Minor chord because the root has been placed on the note B. If you know the names of the notes on the bottom string of the guitar, you can place this chord shape anywhere and play *any* minor chord.

Here are the notes on the bottom string of the guitar:

Notes on the Sixth String

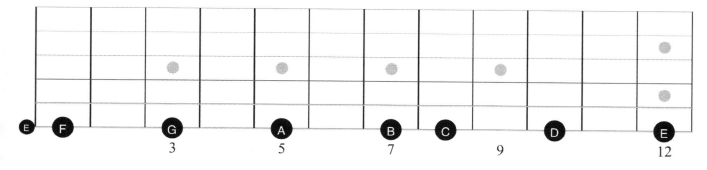

So, by placing the minor barre on the 5th fret, you will create an Am chord:

Example 3b:

A Minor

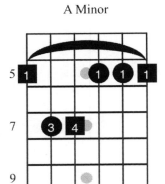

If you place the minor barre shape on the 10th fret, you will play a Dm chord.

Example 3c:

D Minor

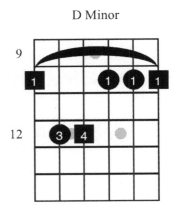

Check that these chords sound similar to their open string versions by first playing the barre chord and then playing the open string chord. The *voicing* of the chord is different, but they both have the same overall sound or *tonality*.

Example 3d:

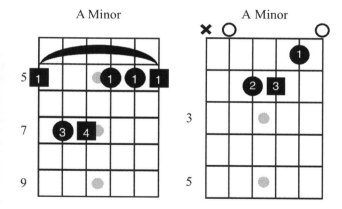

A Minor   A Minor

Use the map of the notes on the sixth string above to play the following chord progression. All you need to do is use the minor barre shape and slide to the correct location for each chord. Listen to the audio to hear how this works.

Example 3e:

Gm   Cm   Bbm   Dm

The note Bb is located on the 6th fret between A and B.

Now you have learnt the Minor barre chord voicing for the sixth string, let's learn the *Major* barre chord voicing.

Example 3f:

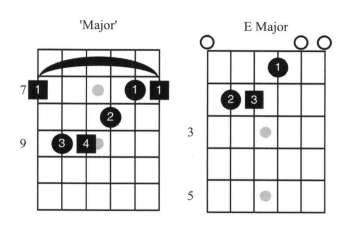

'Major'   E Major

As you can see, this barre chord has the same shape as the open E Major chord from Chapter One, but it uses a first finger barre instead of playing the open strings.

Barre chords allow us to move all the notes in a chord up the neck while keeping their relationship with the root intact. Everything moves in the same amount because there are no open strings.

All we need is to know a barre shape for each chord *type* (major, minor '7' etc.) and where to place it.

Repeat Example 3e, but this time use major barres instead of minor barres.

Example 3g:

We can also play barre chords on the fifth string using the A Major, and A Minor shapes from Chapter One.

Here is a movable Minor barre chord shape with the root on the fifth string.

Example 3h:

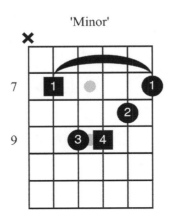

Here is the movable Major barre chord shape with the root on the fifth string.

Example 3i:

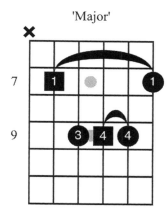

'Major'

The major barre on the 5th string is quite challenging because the barre is not played with the first finger. In fact, there are various ways to finger this chord. Some people even play all three notes on the 9th fret with a third finger barre. Either way, you don't need to worry about hitting the note on the 1st (thinnest) string. It's a bit awkward and doesn't add much to the sound of the chord, so don't worry if it is muted for now.

Once you know how to play the Major and Minor barre chord shapes on the fifth string, all you need to know is where to find the root notes to be able to access *any* major or minor chord. The following diagram shows the location of each note on the fifth string. Notes like D#/Eb are located between the notes D and E.

Notes on the Fifth String

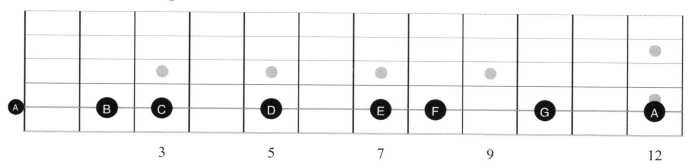

Play through the following sequence using only minor barre chords on the fifth string.

Example 3j:

Play through the following sequence using only major barre chords on the fifth string.

Example 3k:

Play through the following sequence but this time combine major and minor barre chords on the fifth string.

Example 3l:

Next, play through this progression that combines major and minor barres on both the 5th and the 6th strings. There are a few ways to play this progression depending on where you choose to play the barres. You could play any chord with a root on either the 5th or 6th string.

Example 3m:

Try playing through some of the progressions in Chapters One and Two but this time play them with barre chords.

The placement of barre chords can be limited by the type of guitar you are playing. It is more difficult to play barres on an acoustic guitar as the strings are normally thicker. Also, acoustic guitars often only tend to give access to around the 10th fret where the guitar neck joins the body.

Electric guitars usually have a greater available range and thinner strings, making barre chords easier to play.

There are barre chord shapes for every type of chord *quality*. We will talk more about chord qualities and look at a little theory in the next chapter, but for now, simply learn the following barre chord shapes.

Example 3n:

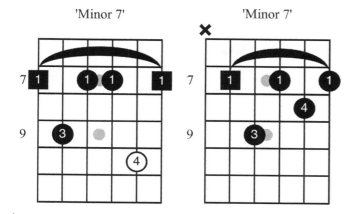

Example 3o:

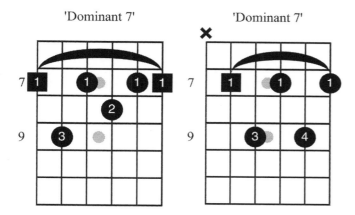

Example 3p:

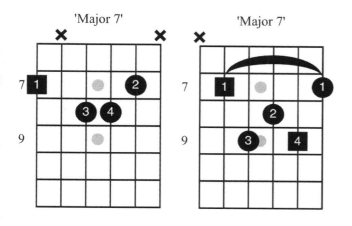

Even though the Major 7 barre on the sixth string isn't technically a barre chord, the underside of the first finger is used to mute the unfretted fifth string as shown by the 'x'. As there are no ringing strings, the shape is movable.

As always, learn each barre chord individually using the steps in the **How to Practice** chapter, before combining different chords into sequences.

Here are some ideas to get you started. It doesn't matter whether you use a 6th string, or a 5th string barre to play each chord, so there are many ways to play through each sequence. Try to keep the chords close together to avoid big movements up and down the neck. For example, it is normally preferable to play Am to Dm by moving a barre chord from the 6th to the 5th string, rather than sliding the same shape from the 5th to the 10th fret on the sixth string.

Example 3q:

Example 3r:

Example 3s:

Try altering sequences from the previous two chapters to use these new 7th chords. Try turning a Major chord into a Dominant 7 or a Major 7th. Try turning a Minor chord into a m7 chord or a Dominant 7th. You can create some great results.

Write down your favourite ideas and you'll be well on your way to some serious song writing.

Chapter Four: A Little (Non-Scary) Music Theory

If you're *not* interested in learning the theory of how music works and just want to learn some more chords then you are allowed to skip this chapter! I do suggest you use this section as a little 'light' night time reading though, because it's good to understand what you are playing; it will help you to be more creative.

In previous chapters, we came across some '7th' chords so let's now learn how they are formed.

Chord construction begins with scales.

What is a scale?

As far as we need to know for this book, a scale is a sequence of notes that begins and ends in the same place. For example, the scale of C Major is

C D E F G A B C

Scales are very important, so if you want more information about how they work, I highly recommend my two books, **The Circle of Fifths for Guitarists** and **The Practical Guide to Modern Music Theory for Guitarists**.

What is a chord?

A chord, technically, is the combination of three or more notes. A major or minor chord has only three individual notes. Often, major or minor chords on the guitar *look* like they have more than three notes. However, even though we play notes on four, five, or even six strings, we are only actually playing three separate individual notes which are doubled in different octaves.

For example, in the following chord of C Major, the names of the notes are labelled. You can see that even though we play six strings, there are only three unique notes.

C Major Chord

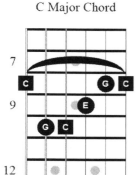

In this voicing, the note C appears three times, and the note G appears twice. The only note to appear once is the E.

Where do these notes come from?

To find out which notes go together to form each individual chord, we must learn how to *harmonise* the major scale.

Chords are formed when we 'stack' specific notes from a scale on top of each other. Look again at the previous example. The chord of C Major contains *only* the notes, C, E and G. In the context of the major scale, we have taken the notes 1, 3 and 5:

C	D	E	F	G	A	B	C
1	2	3	4	5	6	7	8/1

This can be seen as 'jumping over', or 'leapfrogging' every other note in the scale. For example, we formed this chord by starting on C, jumping D and landing on E, jumping F and landing on G. This is how most simple, three-note chords are formed.

C E G

D F A

E G B

F A C

G B D

A C E

B D F

If we view the notes of C Major spaced out on the fretboard, we can establish what pattern of notes is required to form a Major chord.

Example 4a:

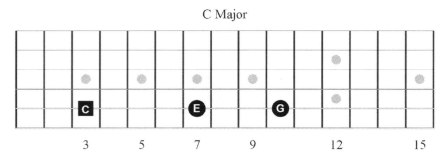

C Major

The distance between the notes C and E is *two tones*.

Any chord with a distance of two tones between the first two notes can be classed as a 'major-type' chord. This distance in music is called a *'major 3rd'*.

The distance between the 3rd and 5th (the notes E and G), is *one-and-a-half tones*. This is *one semitone smaller* than the major 3rd, so we call it a *minor* 3rd.

When measured from the *root*, any major chord *must* consist of two tones between the root and 3rd, and three-and-a-half tones between the root and 5th.

It is the convention in music to describe the notes in a chord in terms of their relationship to the major scale formula, **1 2 3 4 5 6 7**.

So, in simple terms, a Major chord has the formula 1 3 5, and **the first chord of any major scale is always major.**

Moving on to the second note in the C Major scale, (D) and repeating the previous process we generate:

C	D	E	F	G	A	B	C
1	2	3	4	5	6	7	8/1

As we harmonise up from the second note of the scale, we get the notes D, F and A. On the guitar, these look and sound like:

Example 4b:

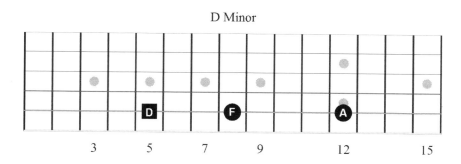

D Minor

The distance between the notes D and F is one-and-a-half tones or a *'minor 3rd'* which means that the chord is *minor*.

However, the distance between the notes D and A is still three-and-a-half tones, which is the correct spacing for a *perfect* 5th.

With a minor 3rd and a perfect 5th, this chord is classified as a minor chord built on the note D, or simply 'D minor' for short.

As a formula, a minor chord is expressed as 1 b3 5 and **the second chord in any major key is always minor.**

All the notes of the major scale can be harmonised in this way, and with the exception of the 7th note, B, they are all major or minor chords.

To save space, I will not show the construction of every chord (although do try this by yourself). The harmonised chords of the C Major scale are:

Chord I	C Major
Chord ii	D Minor
Chord iii	E Minor
Chord IV	F Major
Chord V	G Major
Chord vi	A Minor
Chord vii	B Minor (b5) or B *Diminished*

It is quite rare to play a Diminished chord, so we won't cover them here. In the table above, you will see that instead of listing each chord 1, 2, 3, etc., they are listed by Roman numerals. This may seem strange but actually saves a lot of confusion later. Major chords are shown with capital letters, and Minor chords are shown with lower case letters.

Chords I, IV, and V are Major

Chords ii, iii, vi and vii are Minor.

7th Chords

In Chapter Three, we studied Dominant 7 chords.

In music, you will sometimes see chords with names like 'G7', 'A minor 7', 'C Major 7' or even 'B minor 7b5'. All these '7th' chords can be formed from the major scale. In fact, they are simply *extensions* to the original process we used to construct chords in the harmonisation chapters.

Look back at how we formed major and minor chords from the major scale. We took the first, third and fifth notes by leapfrogging adjacent scale tones. If we continue to jump notes to land on the seventh note, i.e., 1 3 5 **7** we would have created a '7th' chord. For example:

C	D	E	F	G	A	B	C
1	2	3	4	5	6	7	8/1

In addition to the notes C, E, and G, we have now introduced the note B. This chord is a C Major *triad* with an added *natural 7th* and is named C Major 7. Notice how the 7th note, (B) is *one semitone* below the root, (C).

The chord can be played like this:

Example 4c:

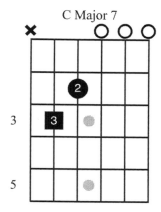

The added note, B is played on the open 2nd string. Play and listen to this chord. Notice how it has a richness compared to an ordinary C Major chord. The formula for a Major 7th chord is 1 3 5 7.

When we add the 7th note to chord ii (D minor), we get the following notes:

D F A C.

This time, the 7th note (C) is a *whole tone* below the root, (D). This 7th note, therefore, is a *b7* not a *natural 7* as in the previous example of C Major.

When we add a b7 note to a minor chord, the chord is named 'minor 7'. In this case, we have formed the chord of D minor 7. It can be played like this:

Example 4d:

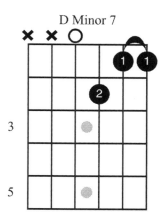

I hear this as a kind of *softened* minor chord. Still sad, but not as sad as a straight minor chord. Any minor 7 chord has the formula 1 b3 5 b7.

The previous two chord types, major 7 and minor 7, account for five of the harmonised scale tones:

Chord 1 (Imaj7)	C Major 7
Chord 2 (iim7)	D Minor 7
Chord 3 (iiim7)	E Minor 7
Chord 4 (IVmaj7)	F Major 7
Chord 5	
Chord 6 (vim7)	A Minor 7
Chord 7	

As you can see, I have missed out chords V and vii. This is because they are slightly different. As you now know, when we harmonise the major scale, chord V (G) is always a Major chord. However, the added the 7th note *not* a natural 7th. Here is the harmonised V chord in the Key of C:

G B D **F.**

The note F is a whole tone below the root, (G). This is similar to the b7th note in a minor 7 chord. What we now have is a major chord with an added *b7*.

This chord is called a *dominant* 7 and is simply written as a '7' after the chord root, e.g., *G7* or *A7*. It has the formula 1 3 5 b7. G7 can be played like this:

Example 4e:

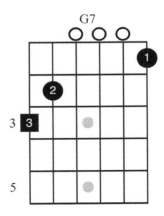

Dominant 7 chords have a tense, unresolved sound, and often move to the tonic (home) chord the key, in this case, C Major.

Finally, when we harmonise the 7th note of the major scale, we generate a chord which is fairly uncommon in pop or rock music but is often used in jazz.

Chord vii forms a *minor b5* or *diminished* chord. When we harmonise this chord up to four notes from the key of C, we get

B D F **A**

94

Again, we are adding a flattened 7th (b7), and so the chord is now described as a 'minor 7b5'. It is often written as *m7b5*. In this case, you would see Bm7b5. This type of chord has the formula 1 b3 b5 b7.

It is played like this and has a dark, brooding quality:

Example 4f:

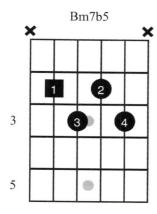

We can now complete the chart of the harmonised major scale.

Chord Imaj7	C Major 7
Chord iim7	D Minor 7
Chord iiim7	E Minor 7
Chord IVmaj7	F Major 7
Chord V7	G7 or G *Dominant* 7
Chord vim7	A Minor 7
Chord viim7b5	B Minor 7 b5 or Bm7b5

You will be very pleased to know there is a simple shorthand way to describe and write any type of 7th chord.

Each has a special formula that describes the way it is formed.

Remember that a major chord has the formula 1 3 5.

A minor chord (with that smaller distance between the 1 and 3) has the formula 1 b3 5.

The following table shows the construction and naming convention of all 7th chords.

Chord	Formula
Major 7 (Maj7)	1 3 5 7
Dominant 7 (7)	1 3 5 b7
Minor 7 (m7)	1 b3 5 b7
Minor 7 flat 5 (m7b5)	1 b3 b5 b7

Major 7 chords are the only chords to have a 'natural' 7th. All other chords (at least for the purposes of this book) have b7s.

To see this process in action, we can simply compare some of the notes in different 'C' chords.

Chord	Formula	Notes
C Major 7	1 3 5 7	C E G B
C7	1 3 5 b7	C E G Bb
Cm7	1 b3 5 b7	C Eb G Bb
Cm7b5	1 b3 b5 b7	C Eb Gb Bb

That's definitely enough theory for now! Let's move on and learn some new chords.

Chapter Five: More Open Chords

We have looked at the most important 7th chords in barre chord form, but there are some really beautiful '7th' voicings you can play in the open position.

Learn the following chords just as you did in the earlier chapters.

Example 5a:

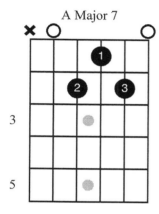

Example 5b:

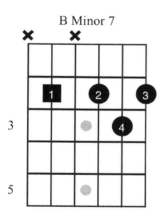

Example 5c:

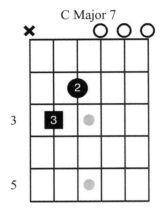

C Major 7

Example 5d:

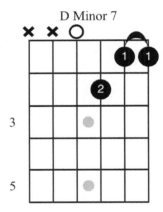

D Minor 7

Example 5e:

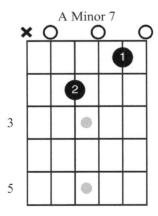

A Minor 7

Example 5f:

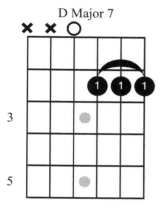

Example 5g:

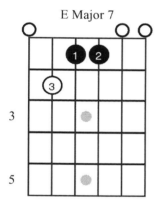

Example 5h:

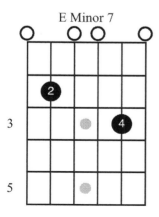

Example 5i:

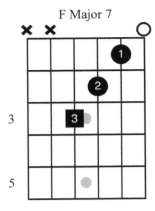

F Major 7

Example 5j:

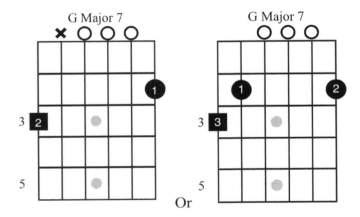

G Major 7   G Major 7

Or

There are also a few chord types we haven't covered yet.

A *suspended or 'sus'* chord is one that replaces the 3rd with either the 2nd or the 4th.

Instead of 1 3 5, the formula is 1 2 5 or 1 4 5.

Instead of C E G, the notes are C D G or C F G.

If the 3rd is replaced with the 2nd, the chord is named 'sus2'. If the 3rd is replaced with the 4th, then the chord is named 'sus4'.

Here are some suspended open chords. Play them and you will hear why they are named 'suspended'.

Example 5k:

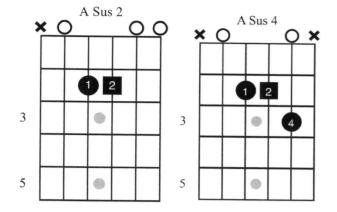

Example 5l:

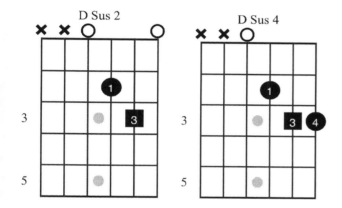

'6' chords have the formula 1 3 5 6. They are quite rich-sounding and a little bit 'jazz'. Often they are used quite sparsely in music as they can quickly overpower a pop-type chord progression.

Example 5m:

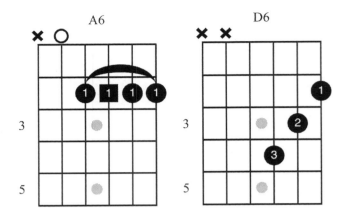

Example 5n:

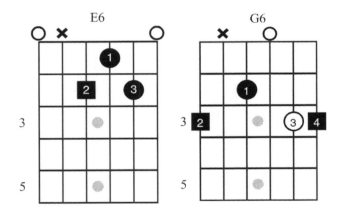

* On the E6, be careful to avoid the fifth string. Try playing the sixth string by itself, then jumping over the fifth string to strum the rest of the chord.

Test Yourself!

Use the following progressions to test your knowledge of the chords in this chapter. Combine these chords with chords that you already know to create new music.

You can also 'substitute' one chord for another. For example, if you see a D Major chord in an earlier chord sequence, try substituting it for a Dsus2, Dsus4, DMaj7 or D7. Not every chord substitution will work, and some might sound kind of weird, but you'll never know until you experiment. Try it, it's fun!

Example 5o:

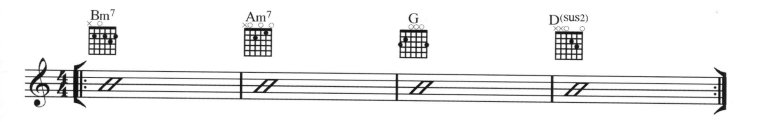

Example 5p:

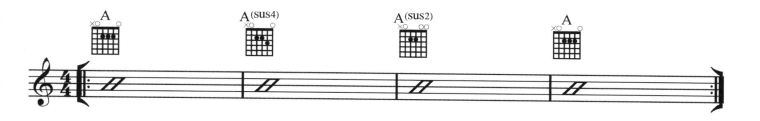

Example 5q:

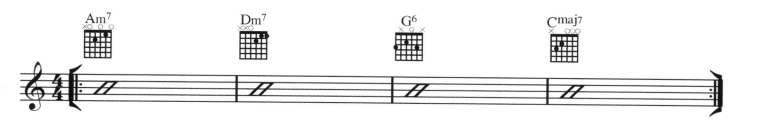

Example 5r:

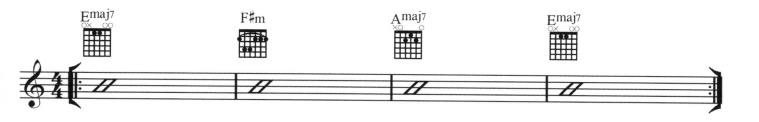

Example 5s:

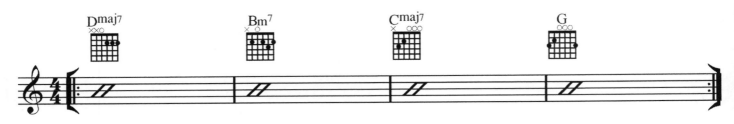

Chapter Six: More Barre Chords

The chords in this chapter are mainly barre chord versions of the Suspended and '6' open chords in Chapter Five. However, we will explore a couple of important '9' chords.

Here are the barre chord voicings of the suspended chords that you should know.

Example 6a: – sixth string root

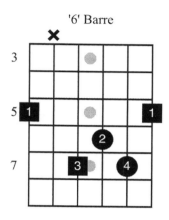

* Be careful to avoid the fifth string

Example 6b: fifth string root

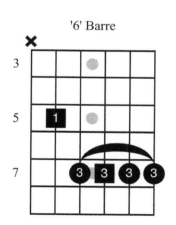

Notice how these barre chord shapes are once again based around the open position versions of the chords.

Next, here are the sus2 and sus 4 voicings you should know. These are normally played as barres on the fifth string.

Example 6c:

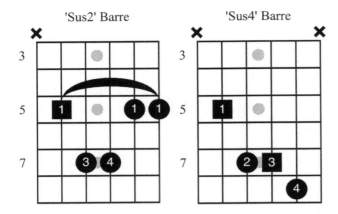

Experiment with the fingering of the Sus4 barre. Many guitarists use a third-finger barre to play the notes on the 3rd and 4th strings.

Next, let's take a quick look at a few common 'Dominant 9' chord voicings.

A Dominant 9 chord is an extension of a Dominant 7 chord and can normally be used as a straight substitution. For example, anywhere you could play a D7 you could play a D9 instead[2].

Building on the ideas in Chapter Four, a Dominant 9 chord is built by extending a Dominant 7 chord by one note.

A Dominant 7 chord is 1 3 5 b7

A Dominant 9 chord is 1 3 5 b7 9

However, we don't normally have to play all the notes of a chord to convey its unique quality. Quite often we will miss out notes like the 5th as they don't really add much to the character of the sound.

Dominant 9 chords are the backbone of most funk tunes, especially anything James Brown-esque. The most common barre chord voicing is this one.

Example 6d:

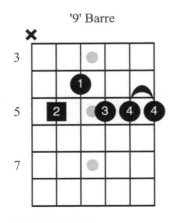

---

2. Handle with care!

There are a variety of ways to finger the above chord voicing. Many players will barre with their third finger across all three of the top strings.

It's also possible to play a '9' barre chord with a root on the 6th string, but it's a bit awkward and less common.

Example 6e:

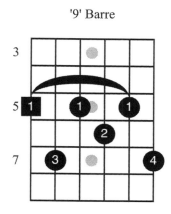

Personally, I'd avoid playing the notes on the 5th and 6th strings, and just aim to hit the top four strings as much as possible. Often it's OK to let the bass player take care of the root notes so that the guitar doesn't take up too much sonic space in the band. A lot depends on context though. If it's just you and a singer, you'll normally need to play the root notes.

Test yourself!

Work through the following chord progressions using barre chords. To refresh your memory, the root notes on the 6th and 5th strings are given below.

Notes on the Sixth String

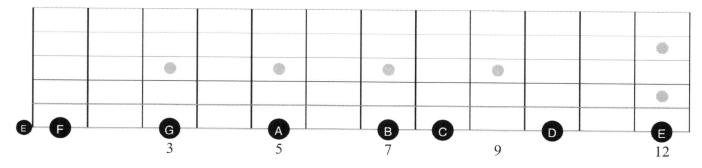

Notes on the Fifth String

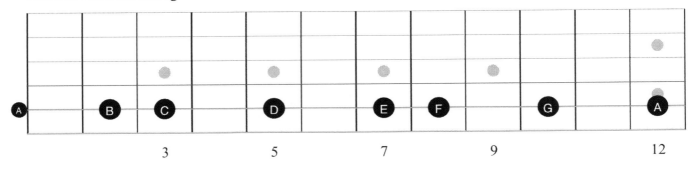

Example 6f:

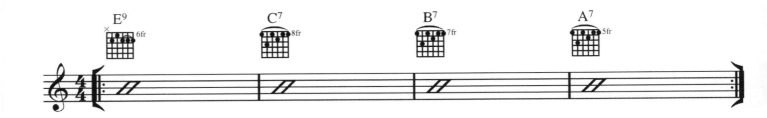

Example 6g:

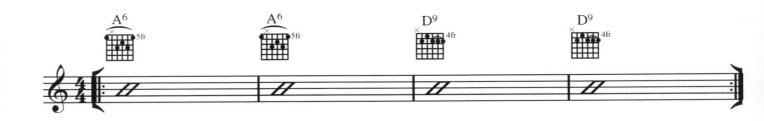

Chapter Seven: Bass Note Movements

When playing open chords, it is common to use small movements in the bass to help link chords smoothly together. The 'top' part of the chord stays the same, but the lowest notes of the chord will often descend or ascend by step. This type of movement is called a *descending bassline*.

It is easy to move between C Major and A Minor by using a descending bassline.

Example 7a:

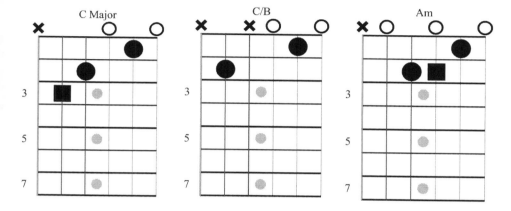

Be careful with the muted strings on these chords. It can work well to pick the bass note in each chord before strumming the rest of the strings.

The name C/B simply means that the C Major chord is being played over a B bass note. These *slash* chords normally sound a little strange out of context, but great when moving between two strong chords.

The same idea can be applied to the movement between G Major and Em7.

Example 7b:

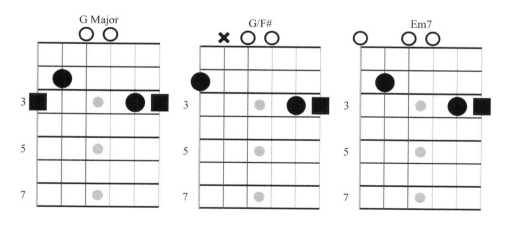

Check out the following examples to learn how you can use these slash chords to create moving basslines of your own. Experiment with other chord types.

Example 7c:

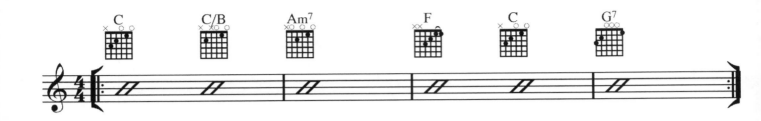

Example 7d:

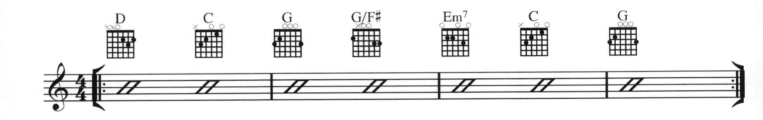

Chapter Eight: Basic Piano Voicings

The chords in the chapter are a little more suited for jazz guitar playing. This may not be your thing, but the rich texture of these chords is great to experiment with.

These voicings are called 'piano' voicings because they mimic the way many pianists voice chords on the piano. Notice that there is a one-string 'gap' between the bass note (sixth string) and the first upper-chord note (fourth string).

The underside of the first finger will be able to easily mute the unwanted string in the middle of the chord.

As always, use the steps in the **How to Practice** section to build your muscle memory and fluency with these chords. Then, add rhythm and start to combine them. Apply these voicings to the sequences at the end of this chapter, and also use them on the sequences in earlier chapters.

Example 8a:

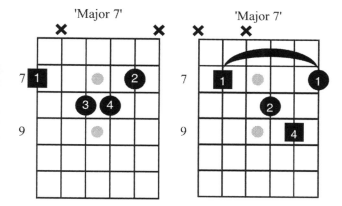

Example 8b:

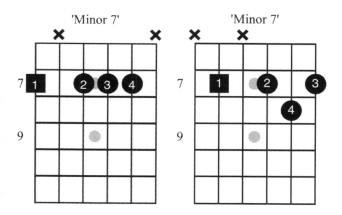

Example 8c:

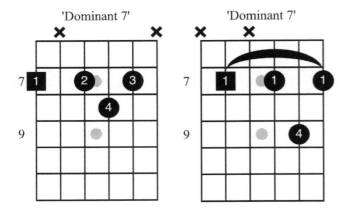

Example 8d:

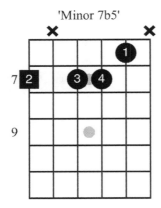

The following m7b5 shape is *technically* correct, but most guitarists will automatically reach for the second, easier voicing.

Example 8e:

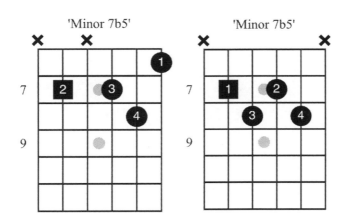

Test Yourself!

Play through the following progressions using piano voicing barre chords.

Example 8f:

Example 8g

Example 8h:

Example 8i:

Chapter Nine: Fourth-String Barres

In this short section, we will quickly look at how to play the most important chord-types on the top four strings. These voicings are used often in Motown and R&B music.

The first major voicing is a barre chord version of an open D Major chord. It's quite tricky to play, so most guitarists will miss out the root and play the chord with the same fingering as D Major.

Example 9a:

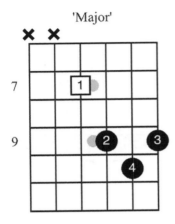

Once again, the Dm voicing is quite challenging, so try playing it without the root.

Example 9b:

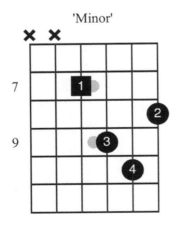

Example 9c:

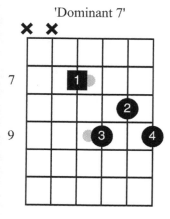

Example 9d:

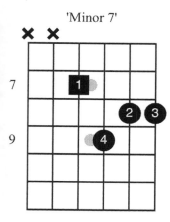

Some guitarists just use fingers one and three to play the following Maj7 barre chord. It's never worked for me, but it's a great option if you can manage it!

Example 9e:

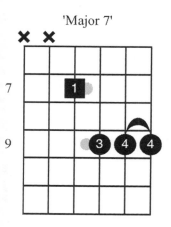

Notice how the following m7b5 chord is just like the top four notes of a '9' chord.

Example 9f:

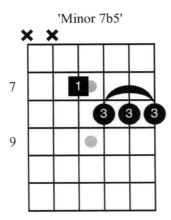

You'll need to know the notes on the fourth string so that you can place these movable voicings on the correct note.

Notes on the Fourth String

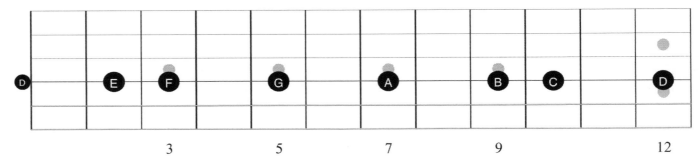

Test yourself!

Combine the chord voicings in this chapter with the ones from previous chapters to play through the following chord sequences.

Example 9g:

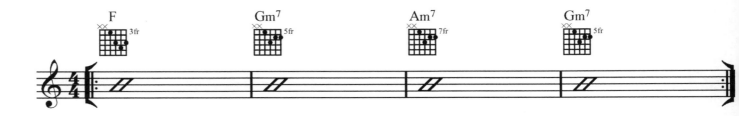

Example 9h:

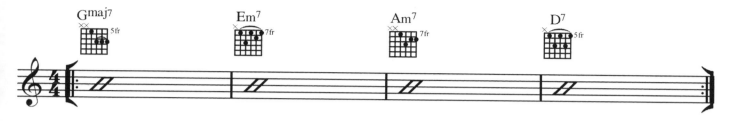

Example 9i:

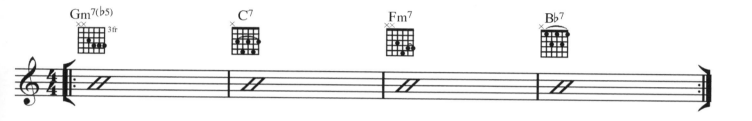

Come up with your own examples and use the four-string barres to play other sequences from earlier chapters.

Chapter Ten: Diatonic Extensions to Dominant 7 Chords

OK, I'll be honest... you probably don't need to work through the following two chapters unless you're really inquisitive about music, or you know that you definitely want to play jazz. If you want to strum out some pop songs, I recommend that you focus your time on the previous nine chapters and apply everything there to as many songs as you can. Spending time in the **How to Practice** and **Strumming** sections of this book will be much more beneficial to you than struggling through this section if you're not ready.

Find some band mates, rehearse, get a gig and have some fun.

However, if you want to peek into the murky underbelly of jazz, you may find the next two chapters interesting. They are advanced, so I really don't recommend them for beginners. Get out while you still can and come back later!

Still here?

OK then... The following section is taken from my best-selling book **Guitar Chords in Context**. It's a constant bestseller on Amazon and goes way beyond being a simple chord dictionary. There's loads of stuff that we haven't covered in this book so I highly recommend it if you're interested in becoming a great guitarist.

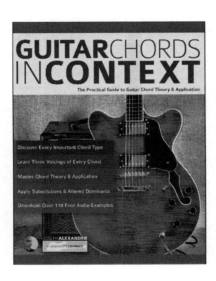

In jazz, it is common to add diatonic 'extensions' and chromatic 'alterations' to dominant 7 chords. A natural or 'diatonic' extension is a note that is added to the basic 1 3 5 b7 chord but lies within the original parent scale of the dominant chord. In other words, to form an extended dominant chord we continue skipping notes in the scale, just as we did when we originally learnt to form a chord.

We can extend the basic 1 3 5 b7 chord formula to include the 9th, 11th and 13th scale tones.

These extensions occur when we extend a scale beyond the first octave. For example, here is the parent scale of a C7 chord (C Mixolydian):

C	D	E	F	G	A	Bb	C	D	E	F	G	A	Bb	C
1	2	3	4	5	6	b7	1/8	9	**3**	11	**5**	13	**b7**	1

Notice that in the second octave, if a note is included in the original chord it is still referred to as 1, 3, 5, or b7. This is because the function of these notes never changes in the chord. A 3rd will always define whether a chord is major or minor and the b7 will always be an essential part of a m7 or 7 chord.

The notes *between* the chord tones are the notes that have changed their names. Instead of 2, 4 and 6, they are now 9, 11, and 13. These are called *compound* intervals

In very simple terms you could say that a C13 chord could contain *all* the intervals up until the 13th:

1 3 5 b7 9 11 and 13 – C E G Bb D F and A

In practice though, this is a huge amount of notes (we only have six strings), and playing that many notes at the same time produces an extremely heavy, undesirable sound where many of the notes clash with one another.

The answer to this problem is to remove some of the notes from the chord. But how do we know which ones?

There are no set rules about which notes to leave out in an extended chord. However, there *are* some guidelines about how to define a chord sound and what *does* need to be included.

To define a chord as major or minor, you must include some kind of 3rd.

To define a chord as dominant 7, major 7 or minor 7, you must include some kind of 7th.

These notes, the 3rds and 7ths, are called guide tones, and they are the most essential notes in any chord. It may surprise you, but these notes are more important than even the root of the chord and quite often in jazz rhythm guitar playing, the root of the chord is dropped entirely.

We will look more closely at guide tone or 'shell' chord voicings in the next chapter, but for now, we will examine common ways to play the extensions that regularly occur on dominant chords in jazz progressions.

To name a dominant chord, we always look to the highest extension that is included. So, if the notes were 1, 3, b7, and 13, we would call this a dominant 13, or just '13' chord. Notice that it doesn't include the 5th, the 9th or the 11th, but it is still called a '13' chord.

As long as we have the 3rd and b7th, a chord will always be a dominant voicing.

We will begin by looking at a fairly common voicing of a D7 chord. In the following example, each *interval* of the chord is labelled in the diagram.

In D7 the intervals 1 3 5 b7 are the notes D, F#, A and C.

Example 10a:

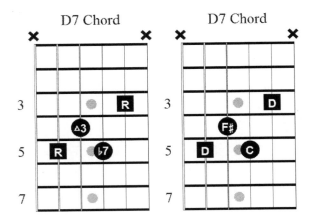

The 'triangle 3' symbol is shorthand for 'major 3rd'.

As you can see, this voicing of D7 doesn't include the 5th of the chord (A).

Here is the extended scale of D Mixolydian (the parent scale of D7).

D	E	F#	G	A	B	C	D	E	F#	G	A	B	C	D
1	2	3	4	5	6	b7	1/8	9	3	11	5	13	b7	1

We can use this voicing of D7 to form a dominant 9 or '9' chord. All we need to do is add the 9th of the scale (E) to the chord. The easiest way to do this is to move the higher-octave root (D) up by one tone and replace it with an E.

Example 10b:

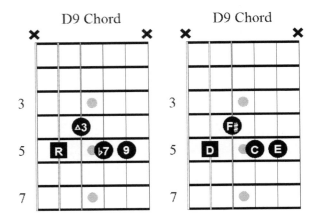

120

Look carefully to make sure you understand how I replaced the root of the chord with the 9th of the chord to form a dominant 9 or '9' chord.

The intervals contained in this chord voicing are now 1, 3, b7 and 9. We have the 1, 3 and b7 defining the chord as dominant and the 9th (E) creating the *extended* dominant 9th chord.

Dominant 11th or '11' chords are less common and need some special care because the major 3rd of the chord (F#) can easily clash with the 11th (G).

We will gloss over 11th chords for now and come back to them later, although the most common way to form an 11 chord it to lower the 5th of a dominant chord by a tone. The lowering of the 5th is generally voiced one octave above the 3rd, otherwise a semitone clash between the 3rd and 11th can occur.

Here is another voicing of a D7 chord. This time it does contain the 5th:

Example 10c:

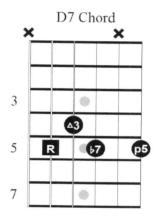

By lowering the 5th (A) by a tone to the 11th (G), we form a dominant 11 or '11' chord.

Example 10d:

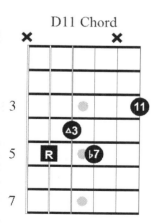

Dominant 13 chords are much more common in jazz than dominant 11 chords. They are normally created by raising the 5th of a dominant 7 chord by one tone so that it becomes the 13th (6th). It is common to include the 9th of the scale in a 13th chord, but it is by no means necessary.

By combining the last two ideas we can form a D9 chord with the fifth on the 1st string of the guitar:

Example 10e:

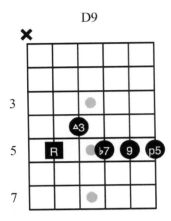

By raising the 5th by one tone, we can reach the 13th degree (interval) of the scale. The chord is given first with the intervals shown, and then with the recommended fingering:

Example 10f:

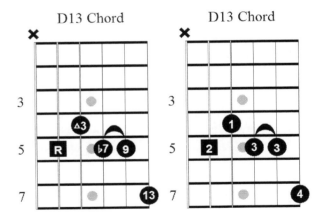

As I'm sure you're starting to see, adding extensions to dominant chords is simply a case of knowing where the desired extension is located on the fretboard and then moving a nonessential chord tone to that location.

The above 13 chord can also be voiced slightly differently to achieve a subtly different flavour. We could replace the 9th with the 3rd:

Example 10g:

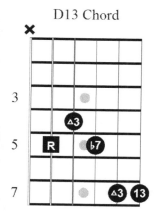

D13 Chord

In this voicing, there are two 3rds which is completely acceptable. You will probably find the preceding version with the 9th included to be a slightly richer sound.

This approach can also be applied to a dominant 7 chord voiced from the 6th string of the guitar. Here is the root, 3 and b7 of a D7 chord with a 6th string root:

Example 10h:

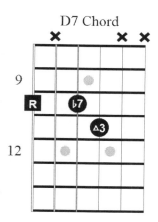

D7 Chord

The 5th and higher octave root of this chord are located here:

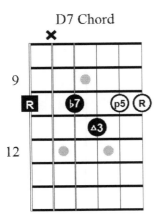

D7 Chord

If you remember, we can raise the 5th by a tone to play the 13th of the chord, and we can raise the root of the chord by a tone to target the 9th.

Example 10i:

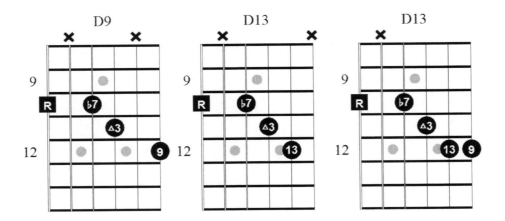

The third diagram shows a 13 chord which includes the 9th. It is still a 13th chord whether or not the 9th is present. The following two 'shell' voicings are extremely useful fingerings to know, as it is easy to add extensions to them while keeping the root of the chord in the bass. However, as you will learn in Chapter Fourteen, diatonic extensions are often added by the clever use of chord *substitutions* that replace the original chord.

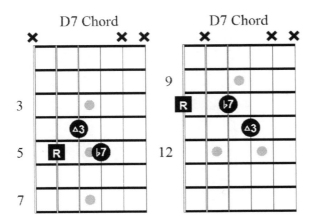

Chapter Eleven: Chromatic Alterations to Dominant Chords

While diatonic extensions (9, 11 and 13) are added to a dominant chord, it is also extremely common to add *altered* or *chromatic* extensions to a dominant chord. These alterations occur mainly at points of tension in a jazz progression, such as the dominant chord in a ii V I (two, five, one) sequence.

A chromatic alteration is a note that is added to a dominant chord that is not a 9, 11 or 13. We can account for *every* possible chromatic alteration by simply raising or flattening the 9th or 5th of the chord. In fact, there are only really four possible altered extensions; b5, #5, b9 and #9.

To see why this is true, let's look at a little bit of theory. Here is the two-octave scale of C Mixolydian, the parent scale of C7:

C	D	E	F	G	A	Bb	C	D	E	F	G	A	Bb	C
1	2	3	4	5	6	b7	1/8	9	3	11	5	13	b7	1

And here it is laid out on the guitar neck:

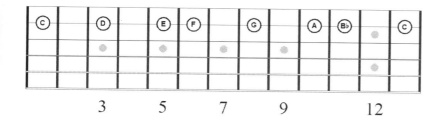

The 5th of the scale is the note G, and the 9th is the note D.

I can sharpen the 5th (G) to become a G# to create a #5 tension. I could also achieve the same result by flattening the 6th or 13th note (A) to become an Ab/G#.

For this reason, a b13 interval is exactly the same as a #5. The chords C7#5 and C7b13 are the same.

If you look at the fretboard again, you will see that a #11 (F#) is identical to a b5 (Gb).

A similar thing happens with the 9th of the scale, but in any dominant chord you would *never* flatten the 3rd because it would change the quality of the chord from dominant to minor 7.

Remember dominant = 1 3 5 b7, and minor 7 = 1 b3 5 b7. By flattening the 3rd of a dominant chord, we change the chord quality so it is no longer dominant, unless there is *another* major 3rd sounding in the chord.

I can sharpen the 9th (D) to become a D# and create a C7#9 sound. I can also flatten the 9th to Db to create a 7b9 sound.

Unlike the 3rd however, it is acceptable to remove the root note from any chord, so as you will see in chapter 9, it is possible to raise the root by a semitone to create a b9 sound.

We cannot raise the b7 of the chord because it would change the chord quality from dominant 7 to major 7.

In summary: b5 = #11 and #5 = b13 so the only true altered extensions to a dominant chord are b5, #5, b9 and #9. You will see chords written down like C7#11b13. This isn't wrong, it's just a question of terminology. The key is to realise that C7#9b13 is the same as C7#9#5.

The reason I teach b5, #5, b9, #9 is because it makes the chords much easier to understand and play on the fretboard.

We will work with a D7 chord to make these examples easier to play.

Here is a fretboard diagram showing the 1 3 b7 shell voicing of a dominant chord in black, and the 5th and 9th intervals marked in white:

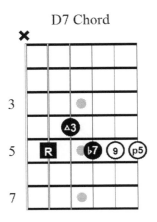

D7 Chord

I can create *any* altered extension by simply moving the white notes up or down by one semitone.

Example 11a:

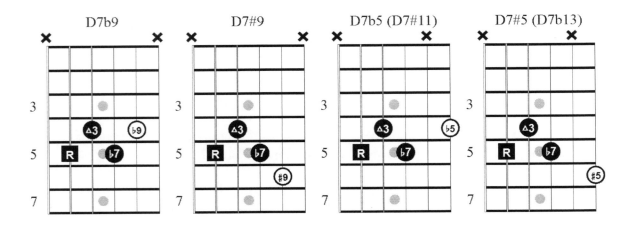

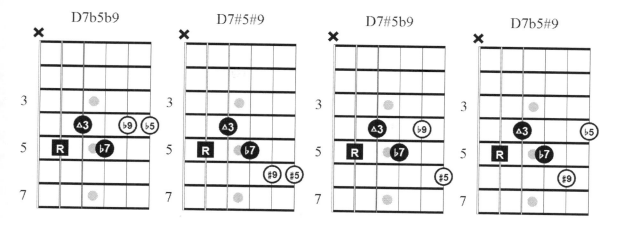

The same is true when we use the dominant 7 shell voicing with a root on the 6th string:

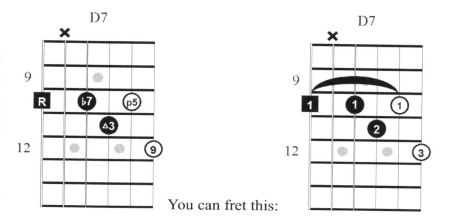

You can fret this:

Some of the altered extensions in this position can be a little hard to reach so quite often these voicings are played rootless. Here are a few of the altered extension permutations available in this position.

Example 11b:

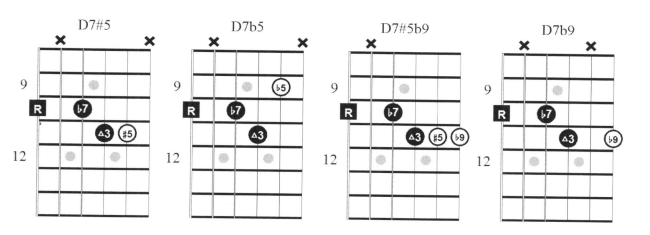

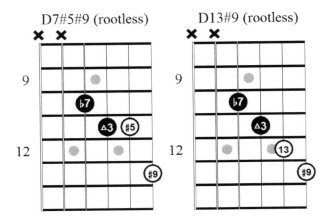

D7#5#9 (rootless)   D13#9 (rootless)

These approaches can be taken with a dominant 7 chord with the root on the 4th string too, although in the basic root-position voicing we learnt earlier, we must omit the root when adding a #9 or b9.

The following example uses a G7 chord as the basis for the alterations.

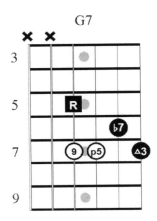

G7

The easiest alterations to add are the #5 and b5, although often the root note will be raised a semitone to create a rootless 7b9 chord.

Example 11c:

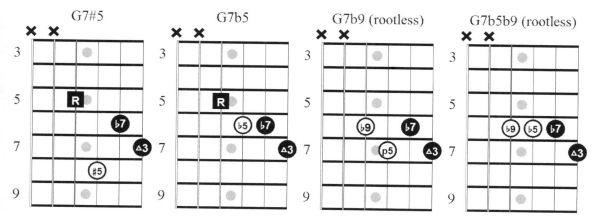

Quite often in jazz chord charts, you will simply see the symbol 'alt'. For example 'D7alt'. This means that the composer has not specified a particular altered extension for a dominant 7 chord and so you can use whichever one you feel works best with the music.

It is also important to know that just because a chord chart says '7' it doesn't mean that the chord must be played as a 'straight' 7 chord. If the dominant chord is *static* (not moving), it is normally fine to add in as many natural extensions as you like. For example, four bars of D7 could be played like this:

Example 11d:

If a dominant 7 chord is *functional* (resolving to another chord), then a basic '7' chord can normally be substituted for any dominant chord with a natural extension *or* chromatic alteration.

A chord progression like this:

Example 11e:

Could be played in any or more of the following ways:

Example 11f:

Am7   D7b9   GMaj7   E7#5b9

Example 11g:

Am7   D7b5b9   GMaj7   E7#5#9

Example 11h:

Am7   D9   GMaj7   E7b5#9

Try playing through the following examples beginning from different root notes, and substitute any diatonic or chromatic extensions you like for the dominant chords you have learned already.

1)

Dm7   G7   CMaj7   Dbm7b5

2)

3)

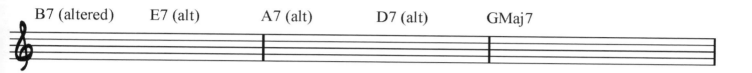

We can take the same approach when adding chromatic alterations to major 7, minor 7 and m7b5 chords. The secret is simply to know where the alterations are on the fretboard.

Chapter Twelve: How to Practice

In this section, I share my favourite techniques for learning and mastering new chords. I've been teaching these methods for years and I have broken them down into bullet point steps for you.

Learning New Open Chords

The following set of steps is designed to help you quickly build the muscle memory you need to memorise, recall and play any new open chord.

1) Read the chord diagram carefully! Ensure you're using the correct fingers on each note.

2) Place the tips of your fingers on the correct notes and strum the guitar once. Don't worry about the sound too much for now. Don't even worry too much about hitting the correct strings with the pick.

3) Remove your fretting hand from the guitar neck. Right off! Touch your leg with your fingertips.

4) Replace the fretting hand and fret the chord correctly. Strum the guitar. Don't worry about the sound.

5) Remove your hand again, right away from the guitar. Touch your leg again!

6) Replace your hand on the chord, and this time pick the correct strings one by one. Listen for any buzzes or muted notes and try adjusting your hand or thumb position until you can pick each note and it sounds clean. You may still get small buzzes at this stage, especially if you're a complete beginner. Don't worry! As your hand gets stronger, these buzzes will gradually disappear.

7) Lift your hand slightly from the guitar neck and replace the chord. You don't need to strum this time. Remove and replace the chord.

8) Remove and replace the chord.

9) Repeat steps 7 and 8.

10) Now try strumming the chord and check for buzzes.

11) If this is one of the first chords you're learning, then take a break. Get up, walk around and grab a drink.

12) Sit down again and repeat steps 1 – 11.

13) Finally, replace the chord on the neck and strum the strings. Listen. Remove, replace and strum the chord. Listen. Do this about ten times. If you know a few other chords, move on to the next set of steps immediately. If you don't know any other chords yet, repeat the above steps with a new chord. The first four chords I suggest you learn are Em, Am, C Major, then F Major 7.

Once you have a few (two or more) chords under your belt, the best thing you can do is to link them together. Our brains work well by learning information and movements in context. Want proof? What's easier to memorise, the words, "Quail, lemon, 78.4, Delhi," or the sentence, "The quail was drinking lemon in the 78.4-degree heat in Delhi"?

Most people would say the second sentence is more memorable because they can easily form a picture in their minds by linking up the words. All we did was add a little useful context.

When we learn chords individually, we are just creating a list of random words. When we link chords together, we learn the sounds and movements in context, so our brains will absorb them much more quickly.

Before you start, get a metronome. It's really important that you add an element of time keeping, and even a little 'time pressure' to get you moving more quickly. In music, rhythm is always king. Your audience will always notice a bad rhythm before noticing a bad note, so it pays to play in time from day one.

I recommend these metronomes.

Metrotimer for iPhone

Mobile Metronome for Android.

They both offer free versions, and it's great to finally be able to do something useful with a cell phone.

I'll use the chords of Em and Am for example, but you can pick any two chords you like. The best approach is to combine the new chord you are trying to learn with a simple chord you already know.

Learning Chords in Context

1) Complete steps 1 – 13 of the *Learning New Open Chords* method for each of the chords you wish to learn.

2) Set your metronome to 60 beats per minute (60 bpm).

3) Tap your foot and count "1, 2, 3, 4, 1, 2, 3, 4' in time with the click.

4) On a "1" strum an Em. Don't hold the chord! Immediately start moving to the next chord in the sequence (Am in this case). You are aiming to arrive there before the next "1", so you have four beats in which to get your fingers organised. If you get there early, just wait.

5) On the next "1" strum the Am.

Example 12a:

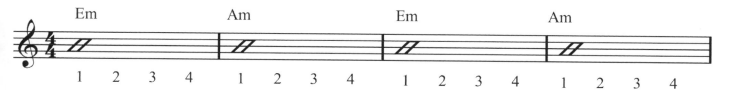

6) If you didn't make it, try again. If it's still tough, give yourself eight beats to get to the Am.

7) As soon as you strum the Am, start moving back to the Em so you can play it on the next "1". You don't need to let the chords ring. Just get moving!

8) If you arrive early at Em, wait and strum the chord on the next "1".

9)   Don't worry about the sound of the chord, muted strings, buzzes, etc. These will improve with time. All you are concerned about is getting to the next chord by the next "1".

10) As you start to improve, repeat steps 4 – 8, but *keep moving!* Strum the guitar on the "1", and play whatever you have managed to get down in the fretting hand. It might sound terrible but that's not important right now. As soon as you have played one chord on beat one, immediately start moving to the next chord.

11) Take a break for two minutes.

12) Repeat step 10. If you're starting to get the idea, increase the metronome speed by 8bpm. Repeat.

13) As you improve, increase the metronome speed incrementally by around 8bpm until you get to around 120 bpm. Continue playing a down-strum on each chord on beat 1.

14) When you reach 120, stop, congratulate yourself, and set the metronome back on 60bpm. Repeat all the previous steps, but now allow each chord to last for just two beats. It will *feel* different, but you are playing the same speed as you were before. Two strums per bar at 60 bpm = one strum at 120 bpm.

15) You should now be playing Em on beat 1 and 3 and then Am on beats 1 and 3. Again, if this is too difficult then slow the metronome down slightly. As ever, don't worry too much about the sound of the chords, the goal is to be in the right place at the right time.

Example 12b:

16) Once again, gradually increase the metronome speed, but this time by 4bpm until you reach 120bpm, or wherever you simply can't make it anymore.

Repeat the previous process but now play four strums on each chord. It's OK if you slow right down for this but keep the metronome ticking.

Example 12c:

17) Introduce some rhythms using the method in the next chapter. Ensure that whatever rhythm you choose has a 1/4 note on beat four so that you have time to change between chords.

The above process can be used to learn, and also introduce any new chord into your vocabulary. Don't worry too much about the way each chord sounds; the idea is to build confident muscle memory first and then hone the movement a little later once you can confidently finger the chord.

Chapter Thirteen: Adding Rhythm

The following section is taken from my book, Beginner's Guitar Lessons: The Essential Guide

I make clear to all my private students that I am not a 'theory first' teacher. I prefer to get hands-on and have them making music as soon as possible. The one exception to this is in the way I teach rhythm and strumming.

Your strumming hand (normally your right, if you're right-handed) only has two useful directions to hit the strings: *up* and *down*. When you understand why certain strums are *ups* and others are *downs,* you build a fundamental security with rhythm. In fact, if you practice the following method, quite soon you'll never wonder how to play a rhythm again. You'll simply hear it and replicate it instantly and unconsciously.

When we talk about rhythm in music, what we're essentially doing is breaking down a song into little chunks. That song might be a 3-minute Beatles tune or a 17-minute Rachmaninov symphony. Either way, we always arrange the chunks of rhythm the same way.

You may have heard the words *bars* and *beats* before. A beat is one pulse of a song: the distance from one click to the next on your metronome. Think of the beat as a one-syllable word.

One beat of a piece of music looks like this:

♩

This note is called a **'Quarter Note'** as you can fit four of them in a bar, i.e., four 1/4 notes = 1 bar.

A bar is a *container* for the beats, and at this stage we will normally have four beats in each bar. An empty bar of music looks like this:

The 4/4 at the start tells us that there are 4 beats in the bar.

If we fill the bar with quarter notes it looks like this:

This is a whole load of preamble to get to one very simple rule:

Every time you see a ♩ you play a down strum.

Down strums are always on the beat, so if you're counting 1, 2, 3, 4 as in previous chapters, every time you say a number you strum downwards on guitar.

Look at and listen to **Example 13a:**

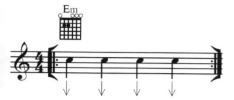

Set your metronome to play at 60 beats per minute, then play a down strum on each click while holding down the chord of E minor.

Try the same idea with A minor:

Example 13b:

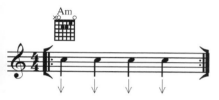

While this is a great method for developing good solid rhythm, music would be extremely dull if all our rhythms were like this.

One way to add interest is to double up on each quarter (1/4) note. In other words, imagine splitting each 1/4 note in half. This gives us 8 notes in the bar, and these are imaginatively called *1/8* or *eighth* notes.

On its own, an 1/8th note looks like this:

But when we put two of them next to each other, we join up their tails:

In other words, in music, instead of seeing two 1/8th notes written like this:

 you would always see them written like this:

You can see that two 1/8th notes take the same amount of time to play as one 1/4 note. So

takes the same amount of time to play as,

That is the end of the mathematics, I promise!

As you can see in the previous example, when we play 1/8th notes, our down strum is still in exactly the same place. All we need to do is squeeze in an up strum between each one. This up-strum should be *exactly* in the middle of each down.

On paper it looks like this:

Example 13c:

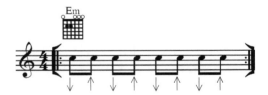

Set your metronome to 60 beats per minute and begin by playing just a down strum on each click. When you're ready, add up strums in the middle of each down. Count out loud '1 and 2 and 3 and 4 and ' etc.

Listen to the audio example to help you.

Try the same idea with other chords like D Major, shown below.

Example 13d:

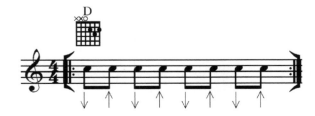

While we have added interest to our playing by adding more strums, music would be very repetitive if this was the only rhythm we ever played. To add interest, let's learn to combine 1/4 notes and 1/8th notes to add variety.

Look at **Example 13e:**

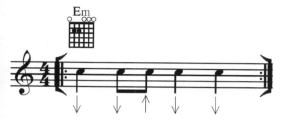

Beat 1 is a down strum, **beat 2** is a 'down-up', **beat 3** is a down strum, as is **beat 4.**

Before you play, set the metronome on 60 bpm and say out loud:

One. Two and Three. Four. Down. Down-Up Down. Down.

Say it in time, rhythmically and confidently. Saying the rhythm out loud really helps your brain to process what it needs to do to strum the rhythm in time.

When you're ready, strum the rhythm confidently. Don't worry about any buzzes in your fretting hand. Ignore them, we're only focusing on strumming.

When you're happy with the above, try the next idea.

Example 13f:

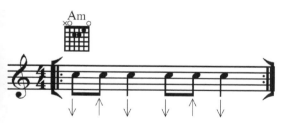

Say out loud, *"One and Two. Three and Four. Down Up Down. Down Up Down."*

If it helps, you might want to think *jin gle bells jin gle bells.*

Throughout any rhythm you play on the guitar, the strumming hand never stops moving. It is constantly moving up and down in time. Downward movements are on the beats, upward movements are between the beats. This keeps you in time, like a little built-in conductor. To create rhythms, all we do is sometimes hit the strings and sometimes miss them.

Here are some other rhythms to practice:

Example 13g:

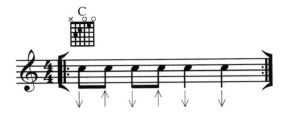

Down-Up Down-Up Down. Down.

Example 13h:

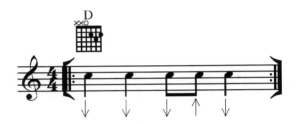

Down. Down. Down-Up Down.

With each rhythm, remember to keep your strumming hand moving down and up all the time. To play a 1/4 note, simply don't strike the guitar on the up-strum.

More Interesting Rhythms

The simplest and most common way to add energy to your rhythm playing is to miss out strumming some down beats. To teach you this idea, we need to introduce a new musical symbol. It is an 1/8th note *rest* and looks like this: ⅞

This rest simply means *silence* or 'don't strum'. It will always be seen in combination with a strummed quarter note so that together they add up to **one beat,** like this: ⅞ ♪

Before, when we played the rhythm ♪♪ the strumming pattern was **Down Up.** With the rhythm ⅞ ♪ we *miss out the down strum* but *still play the up strum*.

To make this easier, always keep moving the strumming hand as if you are going to play the down strum, but simply *miss the strings.* This will keeps you in time.

In other words, the strumming hand is going up and down constantly, but *does not make contact* with the strings on the down strum. This is shown in the notation below by the brackets around the arrow.

To practice this idea, study the following.

Example 13i:

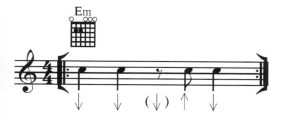

Count out loud: "Down. Down. Miss Up Down".

Next, try holding down an E minor chord while you strum this rhythm. Remember to keep the strumming hand moving all the time, miss the strings on the down strum of **beat 3** but make contact on up strum of **beat '3 and'**.

This is tricky at first, but incredibly important.

Once you have this idea under your fingers, try the next rhythm:

Example 13j:

Down. Down Up Miss Up Down.

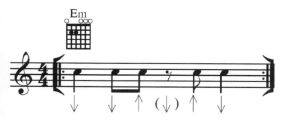

Finally, strum this:

Example 13k:

Down. Miss Up Miss Up Down.

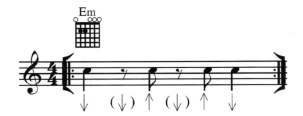

When you're comfortable with the idea of missing a down strum, transfer these rhythms to some of the chord changes given in the early chapters. There is no need to make the tasks difficult for both hands at the same time.

Try the following at 60 beats per minute.

Example 3l:

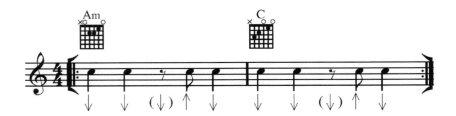

Here's one more example to spur your imagination. Spend as much time as you can mixing and matching chord changes and rhythms.

Example 13m:

Down Up Miss Up Miss Up Down.

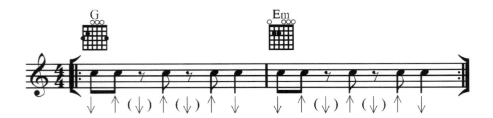

Now try making up some of your own rhythms and apply them to simple chord changes.

Conclusion and Practice Directions

There's a huge amount of information in this book, and there is probably the temptation to try to memorise it all at once. I strongly advise against this, and instead suggest you try to learn just one or two chords a day (or even a week). Spend the majority of your practice time exploring and actually using these chords and voicings.

Remember, context is everything. There's no point learning a long list of information if you're never going to figure out when to play it or what effect it has on the music. While chords can easily be substituted (a Dominant 9 for a Dominant 7, for example), the effect caused by these small changes can be quite dramatic.

In theory, '6' chords function in exactly the same way as straight ahead Major chords, but you're really going to want to know what that substitution will do to the song. Experimentation is the key (and rehearsal with your band too), because the last thing they need is to hear a 'strange' note appear while they're playing. Sometimes risks are good, but normally it's best to try out these ideas with your band *before* you get on stage!

My biggest piece of advice is that there's no massive hurry to learn everything, especially the information in Chapters Ten and Eleven. Those ideas really are quite advanced and I've only included them here for completeness and to give you a deeper understanding of how chord theory works.

If you're interested in what my first guitar lesson looks like for the average beginner, in an hour I would normally have expected to cover five or six chords (Em, Am, C Major, F Major7, D Major and G Major), taught them the steps in Chapter Twelve, and taught them how to strum the first basic rhythms in Chapter Thirteen.

The real work, however, begins once they get home.

I insist that my students practice for a minimum of 20 minutes a day, ideally 20 minutes twice a day because physical repetition is important to build muscle memory. Their homework is to practice the steps I've given them in Chapters Twelve and Thirteen.

If the student practices every day, then normally they come back to me the following week to get some more chords, a few songs, and some more rhythms to work on.

Often, my students develop an effortless command of the chords in Chapters One and Two after about four weeks.

If they've practiced well, the continuing improvement in their ability is exponential because they've covered the basics so thoroughly. At this point, I can write down almost any new chord and they will grasp it quickly. The muscle memory work has paid off by this stage, so all I need to do to teach them an actual song is to write down the chord sequence and strumming pattern (rhythm).

There's no great secret to learning how to play a musical instrument – it's simply a case of committing yourself and practicing regularly. The hardest part is making a lifestyle change to fit in some quality guitar practice time.

Add up all the time you spend on Facebook, Twitter, Instagram, playing video games, watching cat videos on YouTube etc. Reduce that time by 20 minutes and play your guitar instead. I promise you, it's much more rewarding than worrying what Kim and Kanye are up to. Your soul will thank you.

If you need any further help with learning guitar, there are loads of good resources out there.

JustinGuitar is an amazing resource for beginners and improvers alike. He's got a lesson on pretty much any song you care to learn, and his patient, upbeat style makes learning from him a joy.

For more detailed information for beginners, check out the following book. It contains everything you need to know to become a competent guitarist. After working through it, you'll be comfortable with chords, picking, strumming and chord progressions.

Chords are a huge subject and I go into great detail on this in **Guitar Chords in Context**. In this book you'll learn much more about voicings and how to use chords to open up the guitar neck. Three voicings of each chord type are given and you'll learn everything about how chords are created, used and applied.

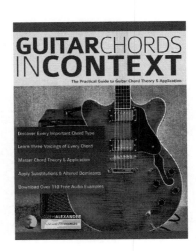

I really hope you enjoy your journey as a guitarist.

Have fun, and keep rocking!

Joseph

Guitar: The First 100 Guitar Exercises for Beginners

Beginner Exercises for Guitar that Improve Technique and Accelerate Development

Published by www.fundamental-changes.com

Twitter: **@guitar_joseph**

Over 10,000 fans on Facebook: **FundamentalChangesInGuitar**

Instagram: **FundamentalChanges**

For over 350 Free Guitar Lessons with Videos Check Out

www.fundamental-changes.com

Cover Image Copyright: Shutterstock

Introduction

I've been writing guitar books for seven years now, and in that time I've been lucky enough to sell nearly half a million books. Throughout that time, I've held to my strong belief that books consisting purely of exercises are a bit pointless.

However, out of the twenty-or-so emails I get every day from (normally) satisfied students, there are generally two or three asking, "What are the best exercises for *complete beginners?*" These requests have been so consistent that I've finally given in and compiled this book for you. However, I'm writing it on my own terms, and on the condition that as many of the exercises as possible are musical and useful to your development as a musician.

You see, that's the problem. There's no point in any exercise that exists solely for its own sake. If it's just an unmusical finger-twister you'll never use, then what are you practising it for?

When hanging out with guitarists, I often see them practising the most crazy, intricate exercises you can imagine; often with plenty of chromaticism and at break-neck speed. They often spend hours perfecting these finger-twisters, gradually cranking up the metronome speed and embedding these patterns deep into their muscle-memory. Admittedly, these exercises look very impressive, but the big problem is that they don't often relate to any particular piece of music. They've spent hours and hours training themselves to regurgitate a pattern that's absolutely no use to them in real life.

Why didn't they just spend that time mastering the difficult bit in the piece of music they were learning? At least then they'd have something to play that'd be useful, musical, and enjoyable for their audience to listen to.

Most exercises only teach you to play exercises, they don't necessarily develop any transferable skills.

For that reason, my normal advice to students is to practise exercises that are built around the passage of music they're trying to learn. There's a subtle implication here, which is that you should be learning a piece of music before you start working on any exercises. When you get stuck, find or build an exercise around the part you can't play, not the other way around.

Obviously, there are some analytical skills needed to figure out what you should be working on, and that's where a good teacher comes in. They'll be able to quickly analyse your weaknesses and 'prescribe' the right exercise to help you master the music you're trying to play. That's also why it's hard to give you an exercise via email. I need to see you play first[3].

However, everything's about balance and there are some exercises that are *always* useful for beginners and improvers alike. These will help you develop rhythm (there's that word again), finger independence, and control.

This book is written for *complete* beginners, so if you've been playing for more than six months then it's probably not for you. We are going to look at the most basic movements you'll use on the guitar and teach you to play them with strength and confidence.

Beginning with an overview of your posture, hand position and how to read guitar music (tablature) we'll start by building your left and right hands independently, before coordinating them together. We'll look at how to use a pick (plectrum) and how to finger-pick like an acoustic guitar player.

---

3. Cue me getting hundreds of videos in my inbox!

Next, we will home in on improving the coordination between your left and right hands, so that every movement is beautiful and flawless. A skill you'll definitely need when you're blazing out those Eddie Van Halen solo in in a couple of years!

You'll find that as you progress and discover more exercises beyond this book, they are often fairly *positional*. This means that your hand will stay in pretty much one place on the guitar neck. However, all the best guitarists make music by moving up and down the neck smoothly. To set you on the right path, I've included a chapter on single string exercises that'll help you navigate the guitar neck fluidly.

There are two very important scales that every guitarist should know, because most music you'll play is created from them. These are the Minor Pentatonic scale and the Major Scale. Not only do you need to know how to play these two essential sounds, you need to learn to break them up into melodic ideas that you can use in solos. In Chapters Seven and Eight, I've addressed these two scales and shown you plenty of exercises that won't just improve your fluency and coordination, but improve your ears and improvisation skills too.

In Chapter Nine, we return to one of the most fundamental skills in guitar playing: strumming chords in time. Believe it or not, almost every strummed rhythm can be broken down into simple units. Once you understand how they work and develop the muscle memory to apply them, you'll always know how to strum any rhythm on the guitar. This is one of the most essential skills you can develop as a guitarist and we go into great detail so that you will be able to play any rhythm guitar part you come across.

The guitar is a uniquely expressive instrument and a big part of its voice comes from the way you *articulate* a musical phrase or *lick*. The final two chapters of this book explore the four techniques that will make your music truly lyrical. Slides, Bends, Hammer-ons and Pull-offs. Each of these techniques adds a different character to your music and when combined help to create your own unique voice. In Chapters Ten and Eleven you will discover the exercises that will set you on the path to becoming a fluent expressive guitarist.

How *Not* To Use This Book

Probably the worst thing you could do would be to work through this book sequentially, one chapter at a time. While I've tried to be as organised as I can with its layout this book is designed so that you can dip in and out of it when you come up against a new technique in your playing. The examples in this book are designed to be played in *conjunction* with your current practise and it's more important that you spend time learning songs and playing with other people than burying your head in a technique book.

Instead, I suggest that you stick to your normal practise routine (see the How to Practise chapter below) and incorporate the exercises in this book into what you're studying for fun. For example, if you're learning your first chords, you might want to dip into chapters three, four and nine. If you're learning a solo and need to build your coordination, then you might want to explore chapters five, ten and eleven. If you're beginning to explore your first scales, then chapters seven and eight will be of interest.

The best thing to do is have a scan through the chapter titles in the index and see what takes your fancy, then build the exercises into your normal practise routine. If you practise for 30 minutes a day, try not to spend more than 5-10 minutes max on the exercises in this book.

This book has been designed for beginners to strengthen their fingers, build their coordination, expand their scale knowledge and get to grips with the most fundamental techniques in guitar playing. All this should be done in the context of learning real music.

If you're looking for a best-selling guitar method that will teach you all your chords and provide a solid foundation for your practice and development as a guitarist, I recommend you use this book in conjunction with my book **The First 100 Chords for Guitar**.

Chapter One: The Basics of How to Play Guitar

How to Hold the Guitar

The most important, and most often forgotten thing that I teach my students in the very first lesson is that the guitar should balance. This is the same whether you're playing an acoustic or electric guitar.

Electric Guitars have a natural advantage over acoustic guitars in that they are designed to balance on your *right* knee which places the fretboard much closer to your left hand. (Reverse this if you're playing a left-handed guitar)

Here you see me balancing the guitar on my knee and although I'm touching it with my arms, I'm not using any force from my fretting hand to support the neck. If I were to remove my arms from the guitar it would remain balanced. This feels a bit unstable at first, like it's going to fall over, but it won't. As you lower your strumming arm onto the guitar it will give some extra support, but the most important thing is that you don't take *any* of the weight of the guitar in the fretting (normally the left) hand.

If you take any of the weight with your fretting hand, then you will restrict the range of movement possible on the frets.

Acoustic guitars operate on the same principle; however, they do not naturally balance – you need to support the weight of the guitar by placing your bicep on the top of the guitar body.

Again, if you were to remove your fretting hand from the guitar, the instrument shouldn't really move at all.

Naming Your Fingers

When we communicate about playing the guitar, it's important that we are clear about which fingers to use.

The fingers on the fretting hand (your left hand if you are right handed) are given the numbers 1, 2, 3, and 4. Your index finger is finger one, your middle finger is finger two, and so on. The thumb is rarely used to fret a note as it is normally planted on the back of the neck, but when it is, it is referred to as T.

On your picking hand, (your right hand if you are right handed) the fingers are called after their Spanish names, but these are always abbreviated to P, I, M, and A. The little finger is so rarely used you'll probably never see it written unless you get deep into Flamenco guitar, but for reference, it is given the letter C.

The thumb is P (pulgar), the index is I (indice), the middle is M (medio), and the ring finger is A (anular).

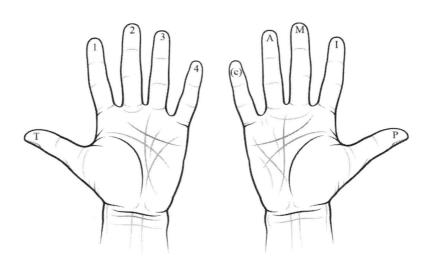

I will tell you which fingers to use when it's important and you will find the numbers written on the music notation above the tablature.

Reading Guitar Tablature

The basics of reading tab are very simple. The tablature *stave* or *staff* contains six lines and each line represents one string of the guitar.

The easiest way to tell which one is which is to remember that the lowest (bass) string of the guitar is the lowest written line of tab. If you lay the book flat on a table, the closest line to you is the closest string to you.

The highest pitched string of the guitar (high E) is the highest line on the tab. On paper, it's the furthest line away from you and also the furthest string away from you on the guitar.

You can now easily see how the lines relate to the strings on the guitar. Often in guitar tab you will see the note names of the strings written to the left of the tab stave, and the word TAB written on the strings themselves.

Another handy way to remember which string is which is to look at the word TAB and see that the B (for bass) is on the lowest line and the T (for treble is on the highest line)

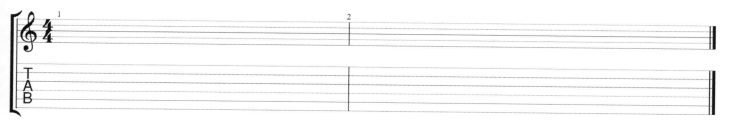

As with standard notation and written English, we read music from left to right.

To indicate that a specific fret should be played on a particular string, we simply write the required fret number on the relevant line.

Example 1a tells you to,

Play the 3rd fret on the lowest (sixth) string.

Play the 5th fret on the highest (first) string.

Play the 2nd fret on the second (B) string.

Play the 7th fret on the fourth (D) string.

Play through the following example and listen to the audio track to check you're doing it right.

Example 1a

To indicate that a string should be played *open* without any fretted note, we simply write a 0 on the required string.

Example 1b

If we need to play two or more notes at once, the fret numbers are stacked vertically on top of each other. Remember, we read from left to right, so notes that are written vertically are played simultaneously. Pick or strum the following example.

Example 1c

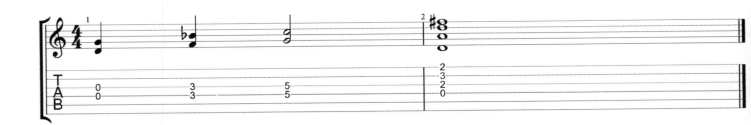

In the previous example, you may have recognised the final chord of D Major. Normally, when a full chord is notated in tablature we add the chord grid and symbol above it to make the music easier to read.

Example 1d

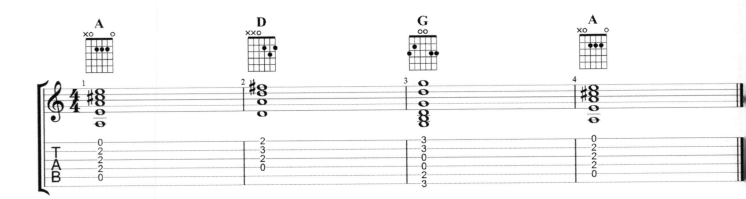

To test yourself, play the following melody on your guitar.

Example 1e

Finally, it's possible to play a note on the guitar which doesn't have any pitch at all. This is called a mute and it's normally performed in one of two ways.

The first way is to gently press on the string with the fretting hand, making sure you don't push the string all the way down to the fret.

The second way is to mute the string as you play it with your fretting hand.

When you pick a muted note it should sound dead and percussive. It definitely shouldn't sustain.

Single notes and whole chords can be muted.

However you play it, a muted note is shown by an X on the string instead of a number.

Example 1f

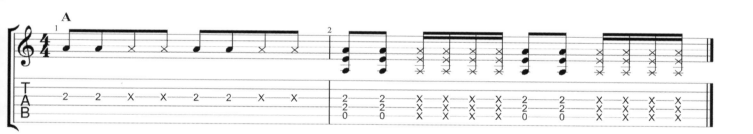

Reading Rhythm

Some people consider that the way guitar tab deals with rhythm to be a bit of a failure. I couldn't disagree more. In fact, when combined with traditional music notation, tab is a fantastic way to show both when to play a note and how long it lasts for.

Rhythmically, the hardest tab to read is the stuff you might find online in places like **www.ultimate-guitar.com**. With these "ASCII" style tabs, rhythm is shown by how the notes are spaced out on the line. No actual rhythm notation is given.

```
e|-----------------------------------------1--3--|
B|-----------------------------------1--3--4--------|
G|--------------------------0--2--3----------------|
D|-----------------0--1--3-------------------------|
A|-----0--1--3-------------------------------------|
E|--3----------------------------------------------|
```

While this *kind of* works if the rhythm is straightforward, anything more complex than simple 1/8th or 1/16th notes can be hard to decipher.

Another evolution of tab combines the rhythm notation with the tab in one stave. Rhythm values are added above the tab line and, as long as you understand how rhythms are written on the guitar, you'll know when to play each note.

You may see something like the example below. Don't worry! You don't have to play this!

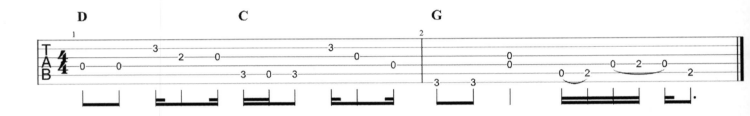

Let's take a quick look at how to read rhythm notation, so you'll be well prepared when you see it out in the wild.

In written music, rhythm is broken down into *bars* (or *measures*) that contain *beats*.

Bars are containers that normally contain four beats. Each beat is split into rhythms that are named according to how they divide a standard bar of four beats.

Special markings are used to tell you how long a note should last for.

For example,

- A whole note fills one whole bar

- A 1/2 note fills half the bar (there are two half notes into one bar)

- There are four 1/4 notes in a bar

- There are eight 1/8th note in a bar

- There are sixteen 1/16th notes in a bar

These notes are written in the following way:

Underneath each note I have shown its equivalent *rest* value. A rest lasts the same amount of time as a note that has a pitch, but indicates that there should be silence for the allotted time.

Notice that 1/8th notes and 1/16th notes have *flags* joining them together. 1/8th notes have one flag and 1/16th notes have two flags. Each time you add a flag the length of each note halves, so a 1/32nd note would have three flags.

Every piece of music begins with a time signature which tells you how many beats there are in a bar. The most common time signature in music is 4/4, which tells you that there are four 1/4 notes in each bar. (We'll take a look at rhythmic values in a minute).

Other common time signatures are 3/4 (three 1/4 note beats in a bar) and 12/8 (twelve 1/8th notes in a bar, arranged 1 2 3 1 2 3 1 2 3 1 2 3). 12/8 is the time signature of most blues tunes.

In the UK, there is a different system for naming note lengths:

A whole note = a semibreve

A 1/2 note = a minim

A 1/4 note = a crotchet

A 1/8th note = a quaver

A 1/16th note = a semiquaver

This may seem strange to much of the rest of the world, but our system does have one big advantage compared to the international system: the metric note names of the US system are all based on the premise that there are four beats in every bar.

However, music isn't always written in 4/4 time (four beats in the bar) – you can have 3/4 time, 6/8 time or even 17/16 time. In anything other than 4/4 time there are not four 1/4 notes in the bar.

The US system does, however, work very well if we ignore this pedantic fact. It is modern, logical, easier to remember and doesn't involve learning quaint English words!

When 1/8th notes and 1/16th notes are combined, we join their tails together. Play or clap through the following rhythms. You can hear them on the audio tracks so listen as you play.

Example 1g

Note Groupings

1/8th notes and 1/16th notes can be grouped in any mathematical combination as long as we don't exceed a total of four 1/16th notes in a beat. They can be grouped in the following ways.

Example 1h

Tap your foot with a metronome and learn to recognise and *feel* the sound and effect of these rhythms.

Any of the notes in the above examples can be replaced with a corresponding rest value.

Tied Rhythms

It is possible to *tie* two notes together. When you see a tied note, you do not play the second note in the grouping. The first note is held for the value of the second note in addition to its own.

In written music, it is the convention to always leave a space between beats two and three for ease of reading. For example, you shouldn't really see this (although occasionally you will):

The above rhythm should really be written like this:

The previous two examples sound identical, but the second example is written correctly as it uses a tie to clearly show where the middle of the bar is.

If we can show the gap between one beat and another then it is normally easier to read. I would prefer to see this…

…rather than this…

Example 1i

…because, once again, the gaps between beats are shown. This is a matter of personal preference and the notation shown in the second line is often used.

Try clapping through this example that uses tied 1/16th notes.

Example 1j

Dotted Rhythms

You will often see a small dot written after a note. The dot is a rhythmic instruction to *add half of the note value again.*

For example, if we have a note that lasts for 2 beats, and we add half of the original note value again (half of 2 = 1), we end up with a note that lasts three beats.

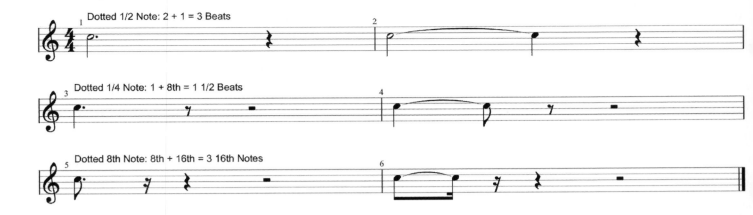

In each of the above examples you can see how adding a dot to a note value affects its length. In the second bar of each line you can see how adding a dot is mathematically the same as tying the original note to one half of its length.

Normally, the note after the dotted note will make the dotted note "add up" to a whole number of beats. For example:

Example 1k

Triplets

A triplet is simply three notes squeezed evenly into the space of two notes. They are written in a group with the number "3" above them.

When learning 1/8th note triplets it can help to say "trip-er-let trip-er-let" out loud, in time with the metronome. Make sure each "trip" coincides accurately with the metronome click. The top line in each example shows the triplet; the bottom line is just there for reference and shows where the original note value lies.

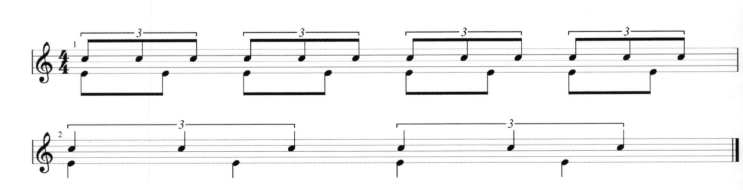

I could write a whole book on rhythms for guitar (in fact, check out my book *Sight Reading Mastery for Guitar* where I stole these examples from), but it's a bit of a rabbit hole and we've covered most of the rhythms you'll come across in modern guitar playing.

So how does all this look in tablature?

When rhythm notation is combined with tablature into one *system* (line), the note heads are removed and the remaining stems float above each note in the tab.

For example, here's a simple example that combines 1/4, 1/8th and 1/16th notes.

Example 1l

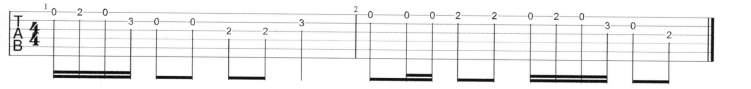

Here's a slightly more complex example that introduces a triplet and a dotted note.

Example 1m

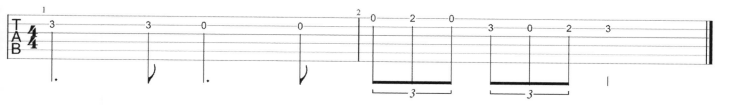

Combining tab and notation into a single line is certainly a great way to save space and clearly shows the rhythmic phrasing of each note. It's certainly a step up from the ASCII-style tab shown earlier.

However, in professional publications, you will normally see both the tablature *and* the traditional notation joined together into one line. When this happens, all the rhythmic information is included in the notation part only.

While it may seem strange to split your focus between two lines of music, this is actually a far better system than the combined tab + rhythm staff.

First, this system appeals to guitarists who don't read tab, but more importantly it allows us to cleanly add much more information to the score. This information may include things like right-hand picking, left-hand fingering, tempo, performance directions and positional information.

Here's a short example of the combined score for guitarists. Notice that the rhythm is included on the notation part and the tab part is "clean". The rhythmic spacing of notes in the tab part directly aligns with the rhythmic spacing of the notation.

Example 1n

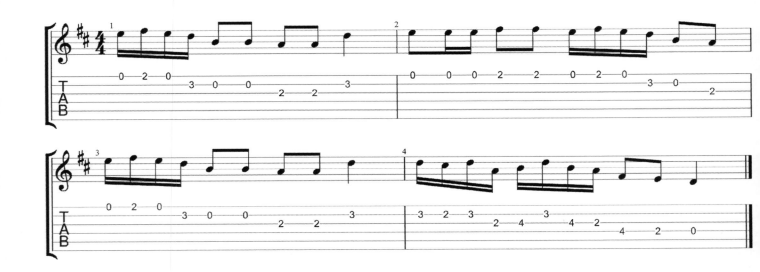

Now you've mastered the basics of reading guitar tab and rhythm, let's learn what makes for a good practice session and how you can more effectively learn how to play guitar.

How to Practise Healthily

There's a real art to getting the most out of a practice session and it is all a question of balance.

First of all, you need to ask yourself what are your goals for playing the guitar. Do you want to strum out a few songs, play a bit of blues, or solo like Jimi Hendrix? All of these are good *long term* goals and they will naturally change as your discover new music and become better at playing.

Long term goals are a great inspiration, but become frustrating if they're not split up into medium and short term goals too. Medium goals give you a sense of where you're going over the next few months and short term goals give you a sense of what you should be achieving in the next few days or weeks. Without short term goals you will never experience a regular sense of progression and improvement in your life and completing multiple short term goals is much more inspiring than only focusing on the long term goal.

For a beginner, long, medium and short term goals could look something like this:

Long term goal: Play a complete song with no mistakes

Medium term goal: Master the chords and strumming pattern

Short term goal: Smoothly change from Em to Am without any buzzes

Short term goals are completed and change regularly and give you a sense of healthy progression in your studies.

As you get better, you'll find that what used to be a medium, or even a long term goal, can become a short term goal.

When you're a beginner, changing between chords can be a struggle, but believe it or not, good guitarists can learn a complete song and play perfectly in minutes.

You probably remember when you first learnt to write, that joining up individual letters correctly was a short term goal. Now, you might think that writing a 2000 word essay is a short term goal because you've already mastered the skills of writing.

All this is to say that as you improve as a musician, your goals as a player will naturally evolve and change.

The secret for successful practise and development on the guitar (or indeed with any skill) is to keep a practice diary. Write down your goals and be honest with yourself. Where do you want to be in a year? Where do you want to be in a month, a week, or in the next hour?

Now you have your practice framework defined, it's time to look at how to balance your actual practice session.

The golden rule is to split your time effectively. Be honest with yourself about how much time you can *regularly* devote to practice. Playing every day for a short period of time is the best way to progress as a musician, so set aside a time that's just for you and your guitar. Leave the cell phone outside the room so you don't get distracted on Instagram.

All you need as a beginner is to carve a regular 20 minute session into every day at a time when you're alert and effective. Spend 1/3rd of your session on technical exercises and 2/3rds learning a song or chords that will actually lead you to play music.

Always play with a metronome clicking. A good slow starting speed for most things is approximately 50bpm (beats per minute), however the gaps between the clicks can often be a bit wide and hard to judge when it's that slow. Try doubling the speed of the metronome to 100bpm and hearing two clicks for one beat if you struggle for accuracy at 50bpm.

One useful practice tip I'd like to share is, "The three coin trick".

Start with three coins placed on the left of your music stand. If you play through your exercise correctly, move a coin to the right of the stand. Play through the exercise again and if it's good, move a second coin across. If you make a mistake, move a coin from the right back to the left. You're only allowed to speed the metronome up (by about 8bpm) once all three coins are on the right hand side of your music stand. It's a simple technique, but one that'll make sure you are programming your fingers correctly and not ingraining bad habits at fast speeds.

90% of the time, rhythm and volume are your top priorities, but sometimes I might tell you to forget about rhythm and just go for volume and speed. It's rare, but this can be a great way to learn hammer-ons, pull-offs, and sometimes slides. However, once you've developed some power, it's essential that you return to focus on playing the exercise with perfect rhythm so as not to internalise bad habits.

The rule to live by is, "The right note, played at the wrong time, is still a wrong note." Rhythm is king and your audience will notice a bad rhythm much more easily than they'll notice a bad note.

Slow and steady wins the race. The exercises in this book are designed to get your fingers moving correctly and confidently as a beginner guitarist. Incorporate them into practice sessions where you're main goal is to learn actual music, and you won't go far wrong.

A constructive long term goal for any exercise in this book is to be able to play it at 120bpm as written. You may wish to double the speed of a few of the slower exercises as your skills develop, but please don't spend too much time aiming for crazy speed. The examples here are designed to build strength, coordination and finesse, not outrageous Eddie Van Halen solos. We have other books for that and I've listed them in the conclusion.

Above all, have fun and enjoy the journey.

Chapter Two: First Fretting Movements

In this chapter we will take a look at the most fundamental movements used to make music on the guitar. It's really important that you work through these examples carefully because they will set you up for everything you'll ever play! Getting these right will put you on the quickest path to long term success and you'll be rocking out before you know it.

As you know, notes on the guitar are created by picking the strings with your picking hand (the right hand if you're left handed) and that's kind of the engine room of the guitar. The direction of the music (melody and harmony) is controlled by your *fretting* hand (the left hand if you're right handed). The pitch of the note you play is controlled by shortening the strings by pushing them against the fret bar, and the shorter the string, the higher the pitch of the note.

To play a note, normally you will use the very tip of the finger to push the string down just behind the metal fret bar. The closer you can get to the fret bar the better, because the closer you get, the less pressure you have to use to hold the string down. It's just like twanging a ruler against a desk at school!

The one finger per fret "rule" is one that is often broken, but it's a useful guide when you're just starting out. All it means is that if you were to use your first finger to play the 1st fret, you'd use your second finger to play the 2nd fret, and so on.

If you used your first finger to play the 5th fret, then you'd use your third finger to play the 7th fret and your fourth to play the 8th fret etc. You get the idea.

As I say, this rule is broken all the time as you come across more intricate music, but in this chapter I want you to use a separate finger on each fret please!

In the first example, pick the open first string and then place the tip of the first finger just behind the first fret. Make sure the finger is just behind the fret wire, ensuring the pad of the thumb is placed opposite, towards the upper side of the back of the neck and roughly behind the fifth and sixth strings.

With the first fret held down, pick the first string and then remove your first finger. Pick the open string again and then replace your finger. Do this four times.

Next, place the tip of your second finger on the second fret and repeat this process for the 3rd and 4th frets. Your thumb should barely move throughout the whole exercise.

Example 2a:

Example 2b condenses the previous exercise into a shorter, more focused exercise.

Begin with your first finger down behind the 1st fret and use the one finger per fret rule to play through the exercise. You'll find that this one tires you out quite quickly, so go in short bursts and come back to it regularly. It'll really help to build your finger strength and endurance.

Start with your metronome set at about 60 beats per minute and play one note per click.

Example 2b:

Example 2c is played higher up the neck and will help you coordinate all your fingers together into a smooth movement. Place your first finger on the fifth fret and use the one finger per fret rule to ascend through the 5th to 8th frets. Repeat the first four notes a few times before repeating the exercise on the second string.

You'll find that the exercise gets a little harder as you move down through the strings, as the tendons in your fingers lengthen.

Example 2c:

The next exercise repeats the previous movement, but makes it a little harder by playing in the first fret position of the guitar. Down here, the frets are slightly wider so it'll help to build some strength and teach you to spread your fingers a little more when you play. Try repeating the exercise at the 12th, or even the 15th fret to see how smaller fret distances affect your hand position.

Example 2d:

Let's now reverse that idea and descend through the four notes. Place *all four* fingers on the 5th, 6th, 7th and 8th frets string to begin with. Pick the 8th fret, then remove the 4th finger to access the third finger on the 7th fret. Pick that and remove the third finger to access the 6th fret, and so on. Planning out your fingering in this way is an essential part of playing melodies smoothly later, and will become unconscious if you practise in this way.

Example 2e:

Example 2f improves both your sense of rhythm and the strength of your second finger. The rhythm shown below is a *triplet* and three even notes are played between every click of the metronome. Use your first, second and fourth fingers to play the notes (one finger per fret) and play along with the audio example to master the timing.

Example 2f:

Example 2g is similar, yet much harder than the previous exercise because it exercises the third finger, which is a weak spot for all improving guitarists. The third finger shares a tendon with the middle finger and is almost always the weakest and least controlled. Exercises that strengthen and help coordination in your third finger are essential to practise, but do them in short bursts as it's easy to get fatigued when you're first starting to practise.

Example 2g:

The next example also exercises your third finger and introduces a jump from the 5th to the 8th fret that'll help to develop your fourth finger too. Use the one finger per fret rule and play every note cleanly and evenly.

Example 2h:

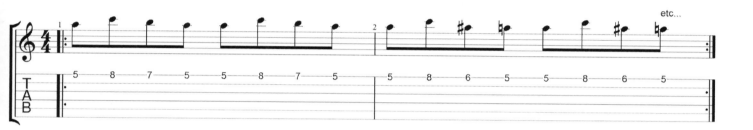

Example 2i is similar to Example 2h, but this time develops your second finger. Practise the sequence in bar one for a minute to two before going on a walk across the fretboard, all the way down to the lowest string. As your fingers straighten out to reach across the guitar neck, the tendons have to work a little harder, so this is a great way to build strength and stamina. As always, practise this exercise in short, slow bursts and keep the notes nice and even. Aim for volume and clarity.

Example 2i:

The control of the movement between the third and fourth fingers is very important to develop but also the weakest in your whole hand. Example 2j will address this, but is also the hardest exercise in this chapter and has the potential to wear out your fingers very quickly, so take it easy!

Fret the 5th fret with your first finger and use the one finger per fret rule to play the 8th fret with your fourth finger and the 7th with your third. The exercise is built around the repeated fingering pattern "1 4 3 4" and will fatigue you quickly. Learn this movement on the first string only, before taking the whole pattern across each string in turn.

You can modify this exercise so you play the pattern four times on each string, or just once. Whatever you do, ensure that the movement is smooth, and that every note is controlled and in time. Begin by playing one note per click at 60bpm and gradually increase the speed.

Example 2j:

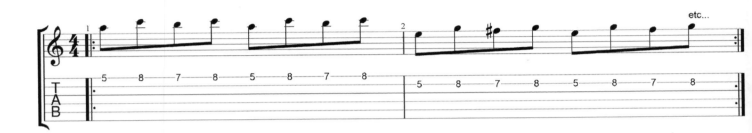

The exercises in this chapter should be introduced into your practice schedule slowly and never take up more than 20% of your practice time – so about 5 minutes of a 30 minute routine. When you feel you have mastered an exercise and can play it as written at 100-120 bpm, drop it from your practice schedule. There's no point practising something you can already do.

In the next chapter we will discover some important exercises that will help you master the coordination and control of your picking hand.

Chapter Three: First Picking Movements

Right-handed guitarists pluck the guitar strings with a guitar pick held in their right hand. Most electric guitarists use a *pick* (or *plectrum*) to strike the strings and there are some important signs you need to know.

There are only two directions in which we can strike the string with the pick: Down and Up.

The symbol for a down pick looks a little like a small letter "n".

The symbol for an up pick looks like a letter "v".

The first exercise in this section is very simple but will give you a chance to focus on cleanly fretting the note (no buzzes) while you coordinate your picking hand to play each note with a down pick. User the tip of your index finger to fret the 5th fret on the G string and play one note for every click of your metronome which should be set on about 80 beats per minute (bpm).

Example 3a:

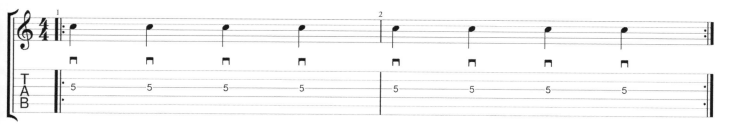

Now play the following melody using all down strokes. It'll build your coordination as you need to change string five times. Again, make sure you cleanly fret each note with the tips of your fingers and ensure there are no fret buzzes. The fingering you should use in your fretting hand is shown in the upper notation part of the music.

Example 3b:

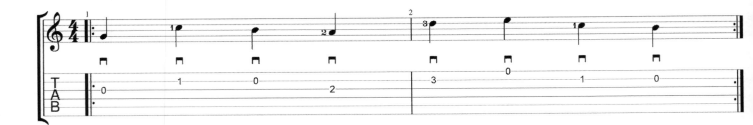

Down and up picks can be used like clockwork to help us stay in time. For the moment, think of every note that falls on the down beat (metronome click) as a down pick, and every note that falls between the clicks (up beat) as an up pick. Listen to the audio and pay attention to the picking markings in the following example. "V" means up pick.

Example 3c:

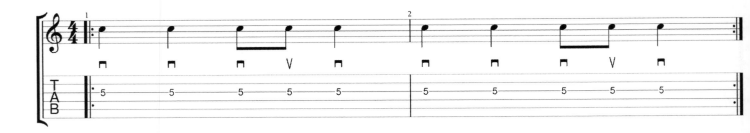

Here's an example that uses down and up picks and changes string. It'll develop your coordination so practise slowly with the metronome set on 80bpm.

Example 3d:

170

The next example introduces 1/16th notes. There are four 1/16th notes in a beat and they are played with a "down up down up" picking motion. Play through this example on one string to develop your picking dexterity before moving on.

Example 3e:

Example 3f is a short melody that I wrote to challenge you. You'll need to play accurate 1/16th notes in bar two and change strings twice. Use the "one finger per fret" rule so that all the 1st fret notes are played with your first finger and all the 3rd fret notes are played with your third finger. Listen to the audio and hum the melody before you play because this will make it easier to remember and connect your inner musical voice to your finger movements

Example 3f:

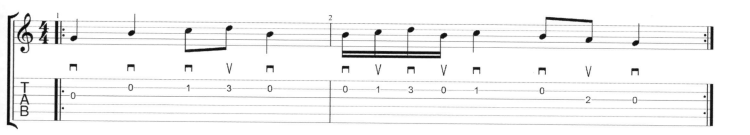

The next example introduces *string skips*. A string skip is any picking movement that jumps more than one string and they are difficult to play at first because it is common to accidentally catch the middle string with the pick as you jump it.

The pick needs to stay close to the string you're avoiding to maintain a smooth movement in your picking hand, but if you get too close you'll accidentally hit the string and make a bum note! Use the one finger per fret rule and listen to the audio before you play. Learn this exercise very slowly as you are programming the fundamental movements of good technique.

Example 3g:

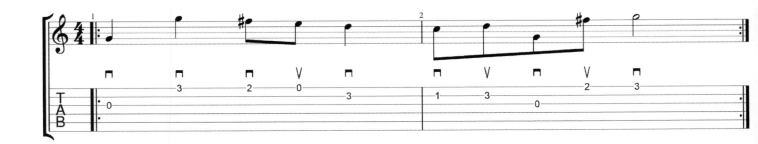

The next few exercises involve holding down a chord and picking smoothly on selected strings. If you've not learnt any chords yet, check out my book **The First 100 Chords for Guitar**.

In Example 3h, hold down the chord Em as shown in the chord grid above the notation and pick on the 6th, 3rd, 2nd and 1st strings in a smooth downward motion. Change to Am and pick the 5th, 3rd, 2nd and 1st strings in the same manner.

Begin by playing the following three examples without a metronome to train the picking hand, but add a slow metronome as soon as you're ready. Skip forward to Chapter Nine if you need some more help changing chords in time.

Example 3h:

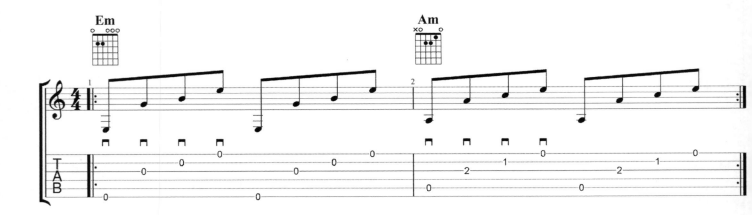

In Example 3i, play the first note of every four with a down pick and use up picks to play the notes on the higher strings. Change between Em and Am as smoothly as possible.

Example 3i:

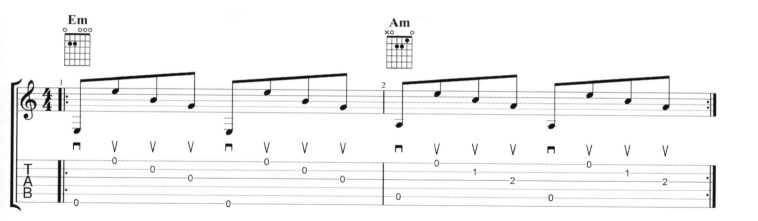

The final example is a little tougher and involves switching between the chords G Major and Cadd9. Look carefully at the chord diagrams and you'll see that only two fingers need to move to change chords.

Begin with a down pick on the first note in each bar, then *alternate pick* the following notes. Throughout the exercise your pick should be moving "down up down up down up down up". This is a little tougher and will develop your picking accuracy in a very beneficial way. It sounds great too!

Example 3j:

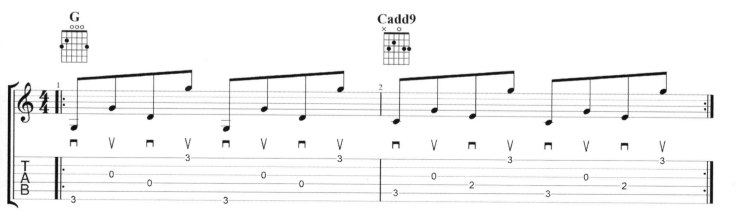

In this chapter we have developed your basic accuracy with the pick. This is extremely important as almost everything you play on guitar is played like this. However, there are often times when playing rock, pop and folk songs that you'll need to use the individual fingers on your picking hand to create rich rhythm guitar parts and melodies. We will study this in the next chapter.

Chapter Four: Finger Picking

You don't have to use a pick to strike the string, you can also use your fingers. As a right-handed player, you use the fingers of the right hand to pick the strings while fretting notes with your left.

Each finger in the right hand is given a name which is then abbreviated and shown on the standard notation stave to show which fingers to pick with. As with many things in guitar, the names of the fingers are taken from the original Spanish.

Thumb (**P**ulgar)

Index (**I**ndice)

Middle (**M**edio)

Ring (**A**nular)

The pinkie is rarely used when finger picking.

In most music, the thumb normally takes care of any note played on the bottom three strings.

The following chord sequence idea (don't worry, you don't have to play this yet!) uses the thumb and three fingers of the picking hand in a classical style. The thumb plays the bass note and the fingers arpeggiate through the higher notes of the chord.

Notice how the letter names for each finger are written in the notation part, but not in the tablature part.

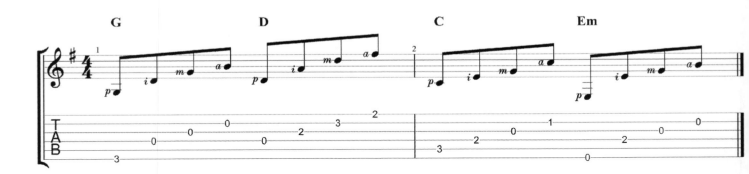

The following exercises in this chapter are taught using the chords Em and Am, but can be applied to any chord sequence you like.

The first exercise involves keeping a steady picking pattern while changing chords with your fretting hand. Use your thumb on the bass strings (6th on the Em chord and 5th on the Am) and use your index, middle then ring finger to pick the top three strings.

Even though you don't pick any fretted notes on the Em, it's important to actually hold down the notes of the chord as if you were.

As there are no fretted notes on the higher strings, you can start changing from Em to Am just before the end of the bar to allow a little extra time if you need it. Listen to the audio track and use a metronome set at 60bpm to start.

Your picking hand should be relaxed with the thumb pointing towards the neck of the guitar and its pad resting on the string. Begin with the other fingers resting on the strings they will pick, and curl them inwards and upwards off the string to create the note. Focus on playing smoothly and evenly.

Example 4a:

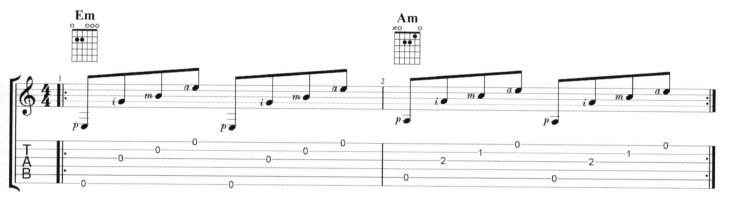

The next example uses the same chord sequence with a different finger picking pattern. The thumb is playing the bass notes in the same order, but this time the fingers pick in the order ring, middle, index.

Example 4b:

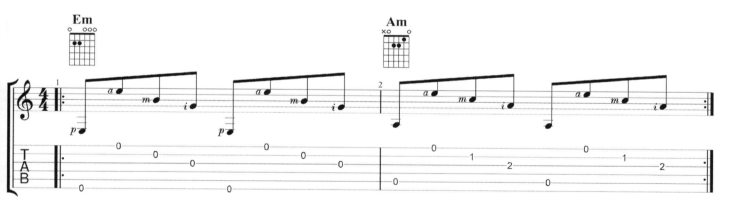

Example 4c is a little more challenging for the ring finger and will help to build strength and control. Focus on playing in time by initially playing one note per click and gradually speeding up to 120bpm, then returning to 60 bpm and playing two notes per click before increasing the speed again.

Example 4c:

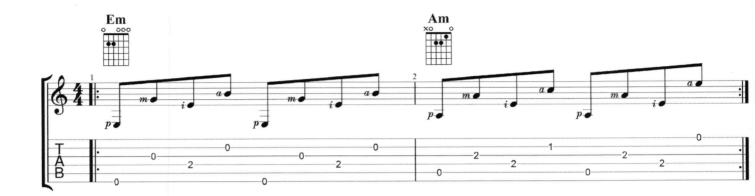

Example 4d introduces your picking hand to playing triplets. There are two triplets in each sequence. The first one ascends thumb, middle index, and the second descends ring, index, middle. This is a common pattern so listen to the audio and practise it until it is completely smooth.

Example 4d:

The next pattern is also played in triplets but is more repetitive and will develop strength and control between your ring and middle fingers. Go slowly and aim to build up stamina over a period of weeks.

Example 4e:

Example 4f begins in the same way as the previous exercise but reverses the notes in the second triplet. Play Thumb, ring, middle, then thumb, index middle. This is a bit of a workout but great for building your mind-body connection.

Example 4f:

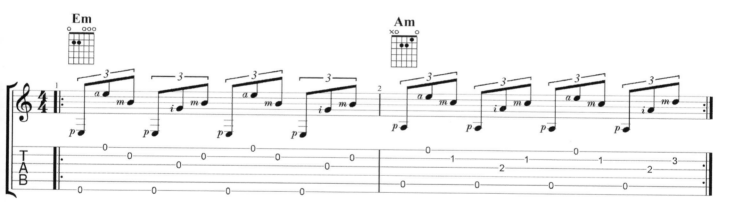

The next exercise focuses more on the picking fingers and develops the often weak movement between the thumb and ring finger. It's awkward to begin with, so go slowly at first. Try this on different chord progressions to hear how it sounds in different situations.

Example 4g:

Example 4h introduces a *tie*. A tie is when two notes are joined together to increase their length. The idea is that you play the first note then hold it for the length of the second note. As you can see, the tie occurs on the second 1/8th note of beat 2, and lasts until the second 1/8th note of beat 3. This is easy to hear but hard to explain in words, so listen to the audio and simply copy the sound on the track.

Ties always create interesting *syncopated* (off beat) rhythms and they're extremely common in most fingerstyle guitar playing. Once you've mastered this example, a whole world of rhythmic possibilities open up to you and you'll be come a much more exciting player!

Example 4h:

The next exercise introduces you to an important thump picking technique: *alternate bass*. Until now, the thumb has played just one string per bar, but now it is going to pick both the sixth and the fourth strings.

When playing in this style, the thumb and fingers are split into two *parts* in the notation line. All the thumb picks have downward facing stems, and the finger picks have upward facing stems. This makes it a lot easier to figure out which digit plays what!

Play the first three notes with thumb, middle index, then pick the fourth string with your thumb to sound the 2nd fret of the Em chord. Pick with your ring, middle then index on the top three strings to finish. Repeat this whole pattern and then apply it to the Am chord with your thumb picking the fifth and fourth strings.

This is one of the most common "advanced" picking patterns you'll come across, so listen carefully to the audio and break it down pick by pick to master it. Go slow!

Example 4i:

The final example in this chapter introduces the idea of playing two strings at once while keeping the alternate bassline going, just like in the previous example. Make sure you're confident with the previous idea before attempting this.

To pick the bass and high strings together, use a movement kind of like a "pinch". Place your thumb and middle finger on the sixth and second strings respectively and pinch upwards to pick the notes. Use the index finger to play the third string, then pinch your thumb and ring finger together to play the fourth and first strings.

Once you have mastered this movement there'll be no stopping you and you'll soon find yourself inventing beautiful fingerpicking patterns on the spot.

The pattern on the Am chord is very similar, but the thumb alternates between the fifth and fourth string.

Example 4j:

All the patterns in this chapter can be applied to any chord sequence. Just remember that the thumb always plays the bass note of the chord first. So, on D chords and F chords it will pick the fourth string. Pay attention to the root notes and you won't go far wrong.

Apply all the picking patterns to the chord sequences below, then try to invent your own picking patterns and chord sequences to quickly create your own music. It's fun and a great workout for your fingers.

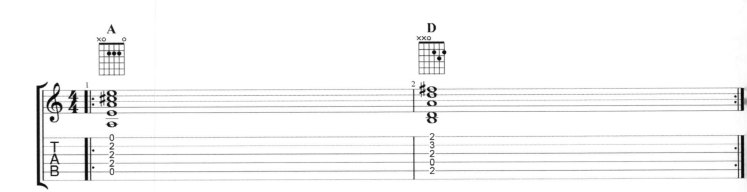

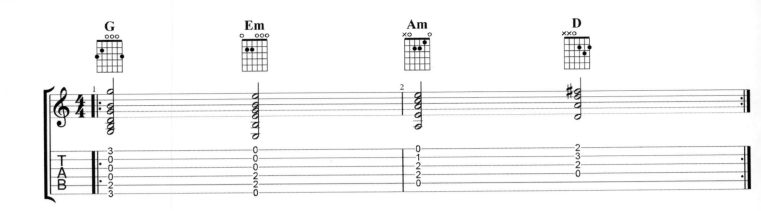

Chapter Five: Left Hand / Right Hand Coordination

The goal of this chapter is to help you develop perfect coordination between your picking and fretting hands and we will achieve this by working through some special looping exercises that are designed to iron out any timing issues between when you fret the note and when you pick the string. Even the smallest amount of incoordination between pick and fingers will negatively affect your fluency, tone and rhythm.

The first thing to get right is your picking hand position as this provides stability and balance to your playing.

Picking Hand Position

It is a difficult thing to explain in words, but the form of your picking hand is crucial. The *heel* (the fleshy part of your hand that is in line with your little finger) should always be in light contact with the bass strings when you pick notes on the top strings. This not only allows you to easily locate the strings with your plectrum, it keeps down unwanted string noise when you play with distortion. If you can't reach the top strings in this position, move your whole wrist lower on the guitar.

Do not anchor your picking hand firmly to the guitar strings. If you want to play un-muted notes on the bass strings, move your wrist so that the heel rests gently on the guitar body. If you were to ascend through a scale across all six strings, your pick should be able to move in a straight line down the strings as you lower your whole wrist. If you anchor your wrist to the bass strings you will draw an arc with the pick which is to be avoided at all costs.

Tuck the fingers you are not using (2nd, 3rd and 4th) away, gently under your palm.

The plectrum should be held on the side of the 1st finger (not the pad) with the thumb gently supporting it on top. You should have about 2mm or 1/8" protruding from your thumb.

Picking Movements

Next, let's examine the two most common ways to pick a sequence of notes on the guitar. The first is with *alternate* picking. When alternate picking, you continually move the pick down up down up etc., whatever the melody notes happen to be. It is a very consistent way to play and great when you're first starting out, but later people often find that it is isn't very interesting dynamically and the tone is too consistent.

You'll see that the picking notation in the first part of Example 5a begins with a down pick, ⊓ followed by an up pick V right through the example.

Learn the following example slowly using the one finger per fret rule. The fingering is shown on the notation part. While you're learning the notes, don't worry about the picking, but as soon as you have memorised the loop, ensure you use consistent alternate picking.

Example 5a:

(Alternate Picking)

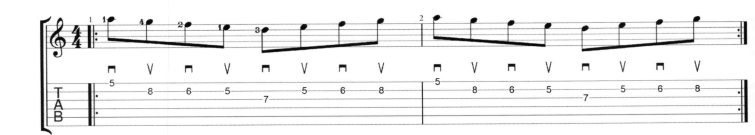

The other style of picking is *economy* picking. When economy picking, the idea is that the pick crosses the strings as few times as possible. For example, if you pick the open fifth (A) string with a down pick and play the open fourth (D) string, it is more efficient to use another down stroke to play it, rather than to cross over the fourth string and then play it with an up stroke.

Economy picking is all about creating the shortest path for the pick between each note.

Example 5a2 shows the identical sequence of notes, but this time played with economy picking. They begin the same way, but the difference occurs between the second and third beat of bar one, and between the fourth beat of bar one and the first beat of bar two.

The note on beat three (fret 7) is one string lower than the preceding note (fret 5), so instead of the pick crossing the string to play a down pick, you play it with an up pick because it is the smallest movement between the two points. The reverse occurs at the end of the bar when you play two down picks in a row to move from the 8th to the 5th fret.

I don't want to get too caught up in the differences between alternate picking and economy picking, except to say that you should use whichever approach feels more natural to you.

If you want to go into great depth on the mechanics of picking, there are two books I highly recommend. The first is **Complete Technique for Modern Guitar**, and the second is **Neoclassical Speed Strategies for Guitar**.

Example 5a2

(Economy Picking)

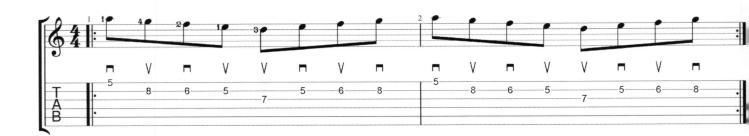

Whether you use alternate picking or economy picking, begin playing through the previous example at 60bpm until you have the whole loop memorised. Listen very carefully to the click to make sure that you are perfectly in time and that you play two notes per click.

When the exercise feels secure, increase the metronome speed by 8bpm and keep playing through the loop without stopping. When you are confident, increase the speed by 8bpm again, and continue in this way until you reach 120bpm.

When you can loop the exercise fluidly at 120bpm, reduce the metronome speed to 60bpm and play *four* notes per click and gradually increase the speed to 120bpm again in 4bpm increments.

While going through this process you may find that you hit a few sticking points or plateaus. Instead of hitting your head against a brick wall, move on to examples 5b and 5c to help you break through it.

The following examples are written using economy picking, but feel free to use alternate picking too. These exercises are designed to coordinate your left and right hands, so as long as each note is played cleanly and accurately, your picking methodology isn't that important at this stage.

Example 5b is the same loop as the one in Example 5a, but it begins on the second note of the phrase. This feels completely different at first, but will greatly improve the coordination between your hands. Increase the speed in the same way as before.

Example 5b:

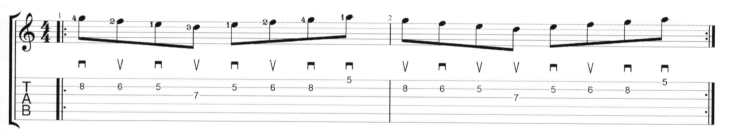

Example 5c begins the loop on the third note of the sequence. Again, this will feel different and exercise your hands in a different way.

Example 5c:

There are eight possible starting points in the previous set of exercises – one for each note in the sequence. Work through all of them and keep a log book of your progress. Give each one equal practice time and try to build the speed of the eight different loops evenly. Practise the eight loops every day and you'll quickly notice a huge improvement in your playing technique.

The previous loop used your first, second and fourth finger, because it is a common pattern when you play melodies, but to develop your coordination there are other important loops to practice too.

Examples 5d and 5e teaches the first two sequences in a cycle that develops your first, third and fourth finger. Work through all eight starting points of this loop in the same way as before.

Example 5d:

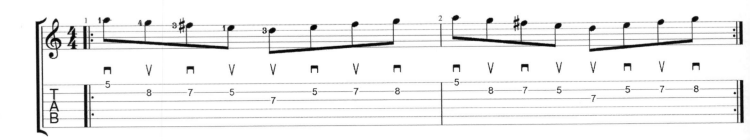

Example 5e:

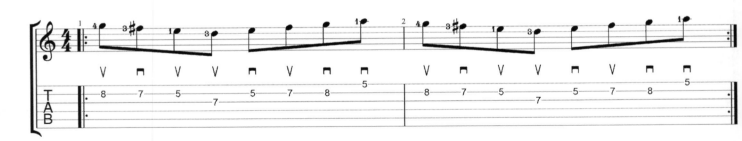

Example 5f and 5g teach you another first, second and fourth finger cycle that has a wider finger spacing throughout. I've written it higher up on the neck, so you don't strain your fingers, but this is another extremely common fingering pattern that's used in many melodies. I've given you the first two starting points, but you must work through all eight to develop your left hand / right hand coordination.

Example 5f:

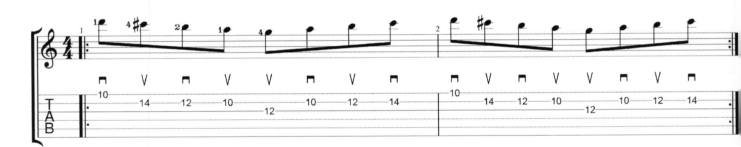

Example 5g:

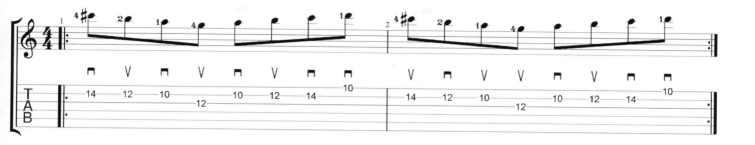

Example 5h teaches you how to coordinate your fingers and pick when playing triplets. Use your first, second and fourth fingers and make sure you gradually increase the metronome speed throughout all six starting points.

Example 5h:

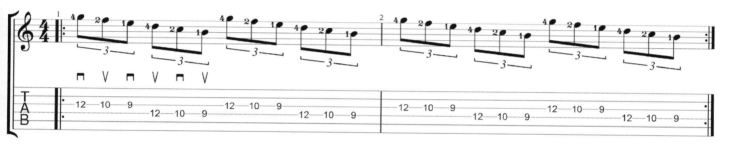

The next example is almost identical to the previous one, but use your third finger instead of your second. It's a lot tougher than Example 5h due to the combination of the third and fourth fingers, so take it slowly and work through the six starting points gradually.

Example 5i:

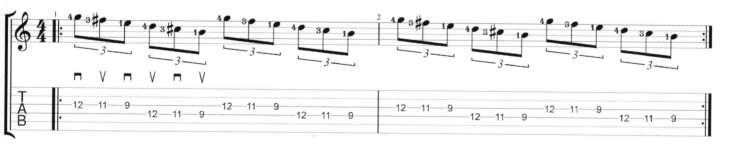

Example 5j repeats the previous two triplet exercises with the spread-fingered shape from Example 5f. This will fatigue you quite quickly, so introduce this set of cycles into your practice routine gradually.

Example 5j:

All the exercises so far in this chapter will greatly increase your finger strength and control, and massively improve the coordination between your picking and fretting. Work on them consistently and you'll see the benefits very quickly.

There's a bonus example in this chapter and it's one that will really test your pick control!

Use the one finger per fret rule to play the following example. Begin with your first finger on the 1st fret of the sixth string, skip a string and use your second finger on the 2nd fret of the fourth string.

Next, use your third finger on the 3rd fret of the fourth string and then skip a string to use your fourth finger to play the 4th fret on the first string. To descend, simply flip your hand so your first finger starts on the 1st fret of the first string. When you get back to the sixth string, begin the exercise again on the 2nd fret.

Due to the spread of your fingers and the string skips, this is a wonderful exercise to build your coordination. Try it with both alternate, and economy picking.

Example 5k:

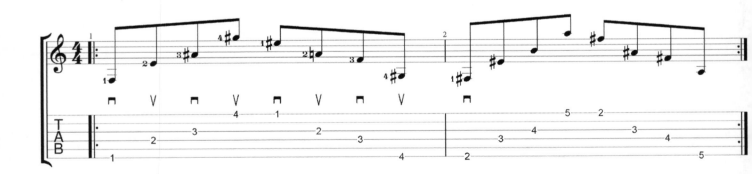

The exercises in this chapter can be quite challenging as every loop is the start of six or eight different loops. But introduce them into your practice routine gradually and you'll quickly notice a huge improvement in the clarity, smoothness and speed of your playing.

Chapter Six: Single String Exercises

If there's one thing you'll find in your guitar career, it's that guitarists like to chunk all their scales, chords and arpeggios into little boxes and section off areas of the neck. In some ways this kind of makes sense – the guitar can be a highly visual instrument, whereby scales and chords can be transposed merely by playing the same pattern somewhere else on the neck.

However, one thing I've noticed after 30 years of playing is that the most melodic, creative guitarists tend to think vertically up the neck. In other words, they "think" *along* the strings, almost like a piano keyboard, rather than across the frets.

Unfortunately, guitar isn't often taught to beginners in this way, so I thought I'd give you a head start and teach you some fun, technique development ideas that are musical and you'll be able to use in your own playing immediately.

We will, of course, build your technique with more standard "box" scale exercises in the next chapter, but for now, let's see how the major scale is laid out along one string.

Play the following idea using whichever fingers feel comfortable. You may wish to use just your 1st finger, or any combination of all four fingers together. Pick the open E string, then a fretted scale note, then the open E string again, etc. This repeating note is called a *pedal* tone.

This pattern of notes will always form a *major* scale when played along one string. Memorise the pattern because it is the most common scale in music. Because it is played on the E string, this is the E Major scale.

Example 6a:

Try playing the same pattern on the second (B), third (G), and fourth (D) strings to form the B, G and D major scales respectively.

Now play that pattern backwards. Even this simple exercise will develop your note awareness and understanding of the guitar.

Try using different fingering combinations until you find what is most comfortable for you. Explore playing the fretted notes in different orders to create interesting melodies.

Example 6b:

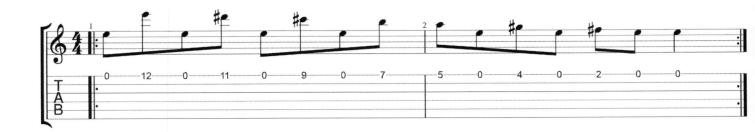

Example 6c is an extension of the previous two ideas and involves playing a descending pattern that gradually ascends the guitar neck. You can see the melody ascending gradually over the four bars in groups of two notes that descend melodically. I'd play this using my third and first fingers for the two fret jumps, and my third and first fingers for the one fret jumps, although you may prefer your third and second fingers. Just use whatever you feel is most comfortable.

Example 6c:

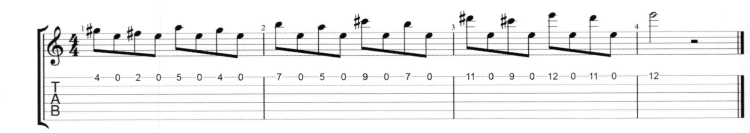

Here's the descending version of the previous exercise. For some reason most people find this a lot harder than the ascending version. It's a great way to test how well you've memorised the scale. Try all these exercises on different strings as they're more challenging when played on the inner strings, since you have to be much more accurate with your picking.

Example 6d:

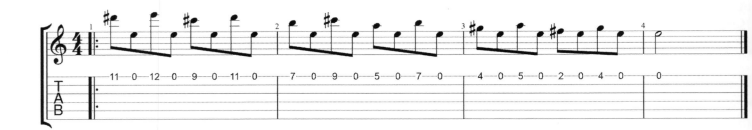

The musical symbol to *accent* a note is >. For our purposes, it simply means "pick that note a little bit harder". Accents are a very important part of phrasing a melody because they act like punctuation in writing.

In Example 6e, you'll notice that there are many notes played on the open string and these can run into each other if you're not careful. The accents help to phrase the melody in clear groups of four. Each ascending note of the major scale is preceded by two picks on the open string and followed by one pick on an open string to form a four-note phrase. The problem with lines like this is that while they sound super cool, they can turn into mush if you're not clear with your articulation and help your listener hear the melody in groups of four. That's why a bit of oomph on the first note of the phrase is so important.

Also, your listener will naturally hear an accent every time you play a fretted note, so you get this cool *polyrhythmic* melody happening, especially when you speed up. Later, in Chapter Eleven, we'll discuss hammer ons and pull offs. This line is a prime candidate for these smooth techniques.

Example 6e:

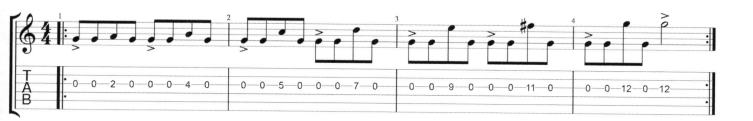

Next you'll learn the reverse version of the previous line. Again, you'll probably find this harder than the ascending version but stick with it and memorise it. Soon you'll be flying up and down the neck like Joe Satriani. Don't forget to play all these examples on different strings to put them in different keys.

Example 6f:

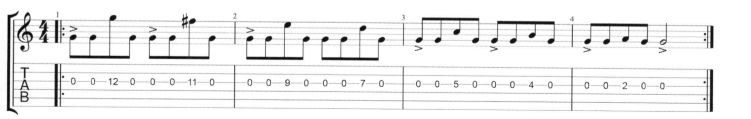

Example 6g is another "ascend as you descend" idea. The general melodic shape descends as you climb the second string. These ideas help you memorise the neck and improve your general geometric awareness of the guitar. Learn this slowly and gradually speed up as described earlier.

Example 6g:

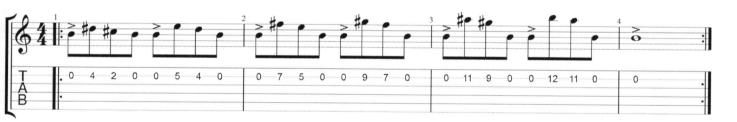

Again, it's important to learn these patterns descending. This time the melody ascends as you gradually descend in pitch. These lines work great at speed, so try to get faster and introduce hammer ons when you need to.

Example 6h:

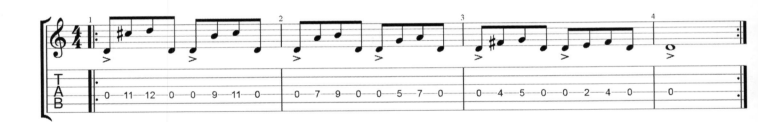

Example 6i isn't quite as exciting but it's perfect for helping you strengthen your fingers. I'm not normally a fan of chromatic exercises but this one really helps you to strengthen and coordinate your fingers. Follow the notated fingering carefully and position shift to your first finger after every time you use your fourth.

Example 6i:

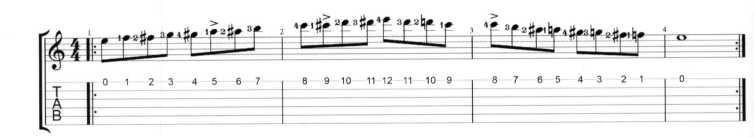

In Example 6j, you gradually ascend the E Major scale using a short melodic fragment. The first note of each short phrase should be played with your fourth finger and you should use the one finger per fret rule where possible. This exercise is all about picking smoothly and will teach you to jump up and down through the major scale along one string. Record yourself playing and listen back to make sure that each note is clean, strong and in time. Let each note flow beautifully into the next.

Play this idea backwards and learn the descending version too.

Example 6j:

All the exercises in this chapter should be memorised and played on all six strings as each string will present its own unique set of challenges. The main problem my students find is keeping the strings that aren't being played quiet. Dial a bit of distortion into your amp once you've memorised an exercise and see if there are any unwanted sounds coming from your amp. To keep unused strings quiet, rest the heel of your picking hand gently on any unused bass strings, and allow the underside of the fretting hand fingers to mute any strings that are higher than the one you're playing.

I highly recommend that you learn to play the exercises in this book with your eyes closed as you will quickly develop a Zen-like connection and feel for the guitar and your confidence will improve massively. Don't worry about any little mis-frets at first. Just close your eyes and trust your ears. Your physical connection to your guitar will quickly develop and you'll fast become a better player.

Chapter Seven: Minor Pentatonic Scale Exercises

For nearly 100 years, the minor pentatonic scale has been *the* sound of blues and rock guitar. Most of the guitar solos you hear are formed from just these five notes and it's essential that you build control and fluency to help you play awesome solos later.

If you have any desire to play rock and blues solos, I strongly recommend that you start learning blues guitar licks as soon as possible and if I may be so bold as to recommend my book, **100 Classic Blues Licks for Guitar**, you'll be well on the way to understanding how the musical language of the guitar has developed, and learning some killer blues licks in the styles of the greatest guitarists in the world.

The minor pentatonic scale contains just five notes, and can be played in the key of E in the *open position* of the guitar as follows. It might feel unusual to use open strings in this scale at first, but stick to the fingering shown and you'll develop the feel in no time. Use your third finger for the 3rd fret notes and your second finger for the 2nd fret notes. Pick each note cleanly and pay attention to the difference in feel between picking an open string and a fretted note. Let each note run smoothly into each other as you can hear on the audio track.

Example 7a:

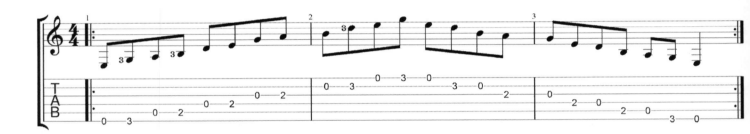

While it's important to know the open position fingering of the minor pentatonic scale, most of the time you'll be playing it higher up the neck with all fretted notes. Here is the scale of A Minor Pentatonic. Use the one finger per fret rule throughout. Notice how the pattern of notes is identical to the previous example, it's just been shifted up the neck. The guitar is cool like that – chords and scales can often be shifted up the neck to easily play them in new keys.

Example 7b:

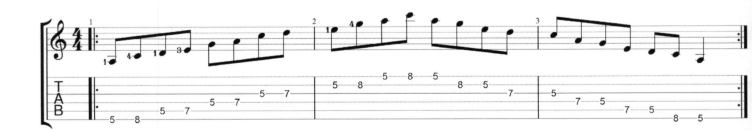

Here's the first real exercise using the minor pentatonic scale. Use the one finger per fret rule and play up three strings of the scale. Drop back a string and then ascend another three strings and repeat this movement. These types of patterns are hugely important and when sped up they formed a big part of the vocabulary of many of the '80s rockers like Paul Gilbert. You need to start slowly because this exercise is all about smoothly navigating the A Minor Pentatonic scale and you should be concentrating on clean fretting, smooth picking and a full tone for each note.

When you have memorised this pattern, work with a metronome to speed up. Again, when you have worked through Chapter Eleven, you can return here to apply all the legato techniques you have learned!

Your fourth finger will likely be the weakest link in this exercise so ensure that each note it plays is as strong as the others.

Example 7c:

Example 7d teaches you a common triplet idea that ascends three notes up the scale then descends one. Accent the first of every three notes and focus on keeping the unplayed strings quiet by using good muting in your picking hand.

Example 7d:

The next example teaches you to think ahead as the pattern starts in the middle of the scale and descends by four notes. A melodic jump and string skip follows each four note phrase, so you'll have to be accurate with your picking.

Example 7e:

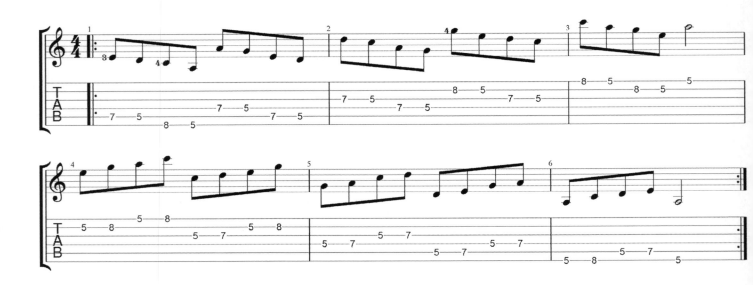

One way to make musical phrases interesting is to create *cross rhythmic* patterns. In Example 7f, the rhythm is phrased in twos (the 1/8th notes) but the melody descends in threes to create a three against two feel. This is a wonderful exercise to practise, because not only does it develop your knowledge and fluency of the minor pentatonic scale, it teaches your ears to hear and apply new melodic ideas in your solos.

Example 7f:

Here's the ascending version of the previous example. While I suggest learning all these examples with the one finger per fret rule, try playing the whole thing with just your first and third fingers.

Example 7g:

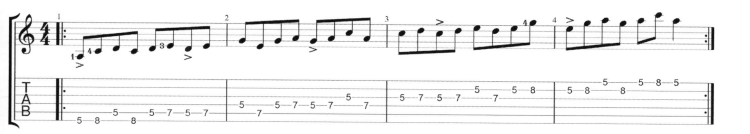

The name for a melodic distance in music is an *interval*, and here is the minor pentatonic scale played in *4ths*. As you will see, each note is played on an adjacent string so this example will teach you to roll your first, third and fourth fingers across two strings.

Use your first finger to play all the 5 – 5 movements, your third finger to play all the 7 – 7 movements, and your fourth finger to play all the 8 – 8 movements. Use your third and fourth finger to play the notes in the second beat of bar one.

Playing in fourths creates an unusual, angular sound and you'll need to roll the fingertip pressure from the lower to the higher string to fret the second note while subtly dampening the first. It's great exercise as this technique is often required when soloing.

Example 7h:

Example 7i is a development of the previous example. Roll your first finger across the strings, ascend a note, then roll back to the original string. The only exception to this movement is between the 7th and 8th fret in bar one where you will again use your third and fourth finger.

Example 7i:

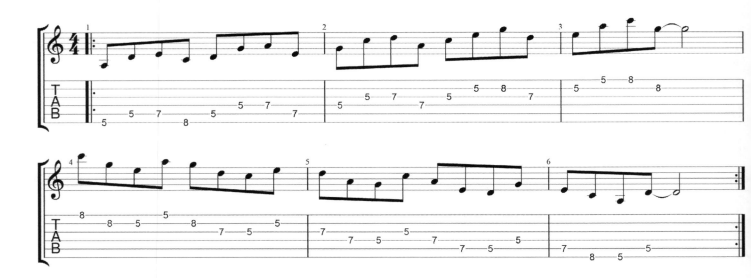

Example 7j is quite tough and you'll need to learn it slowly before building up the speed. It's another cross rhythmic idea that forms a four against three feel in the melody as it slowly ascends the scale. This exercise will teach you to think as well as "hear" ahead more than just a few notes. It's important that you listen to the audio to fully hear the musical effect of this line before you learn it, so that you hear how to accent the phrase. Once you've got it right, it's lots of fun to play fast and you'll use it all the time!

Example 7j:

Each exercise in this chapter is movable and you can begin at different starting frets to play in different keys. Each example is written at the fifth fret in the key of A, but try moving them to the 3rd fret (G) the 10th fret (D) or the 14th fret (F#). As the distance between the frets changes, you'll find new challenges to overcome. Remember, slow and steady wins the race.

The ultimate goal is to use these exercises in the music you play, so grab some backing tracks and see how you can use these patterns to create your own personal melodies.

Chapter Eight: Major Scale Exercises

The major scale is almost as important as the minor pentatonic scale when it comes to writing song melodies and playing solos. In fact, almost every chord you'll ever play is constructed from notes of the major scale, so it pays to know it inside out. The exercises in this chapter will teach you one of the most important fingerings of the major scale and show you how to create melodic ideas while building your technique and fluency.

We will learn the major scale in the key of G because it is nicely positioned on the guitar, but just like barre chords and the pentatonic scale, this shape can be moved up and down the neck to play in different keys.

Begin by playing the G Major scale from the 3rd fret. Use the one-finger-per-fret rule and play the first note with your second finger.

Example 8a:

Example 8a taught you an important position of the scale, and you will occasionally use that shape in your playing. However, the scale is more useful to use when it's played in a higher *register*. In Example 8b you'll play G Major again, this time in upper octave. Begin on your second finger again and this time ascend, then descend the scale. Set your metronome to 60bpm and play one note per click before gradually increasing the metronome speed.

Example 8b:

The next example introduces a common triplet pattern. The idea is to ascend three notes of the scale then descend back by one note before ascending three notes again. You will have heard this melodic pattern many times on TV and on the radio, so it's an important sound to wrap your fingers around.

Set your metronome at 50bpm and play three notes per click if you can. If you're struggling, try speeding the metronome up to 100bpm and playing one note per click. Gradually increase the speed when you're confident you can play the exercise without making a mistake. This exercises are great for teaching your fingers to play the music you hear in your head as they train them to find the melody notes quickly and accurately.

Example 8c:

In Example 8d, you ascend four notes before jumping back to the second note of the phrase and ascending four notes again. Patterns like this quickly develop your finger coordination and build strength and dexterity. Notice that it takes a lot longer to ascend the scale when you play sequential patterns like this one. They're a great way to lengthen the melody of a phrase.

Example 8d:

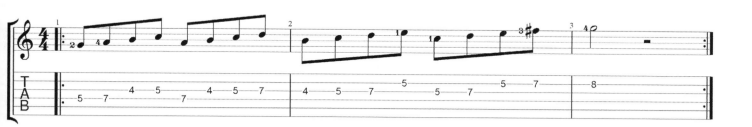

Here's the descending version of Example 8d. There is a tricky moment when you must roll your third finger across the 7th fret notes in bar one to play the melody smoothly. There's also a descending slide in bar two for your first finger that will help you stay in position.

Example 8e:

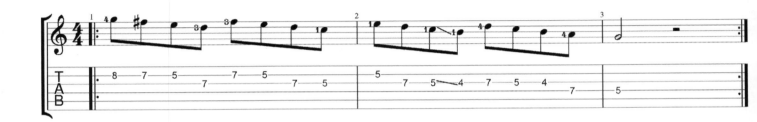

An *interval* is a melodic jump in music. Jumping up three notes is a *third*, jumping up four notes is a *fourth*. In Example 8f you ascend the G Major scale in thirds by jumping three notes, descending to the second note that you skipped, then jumping up a third again. This is a strong melodic idea and will help you to develop your fluency and understanding of the scale because you have to visualise where the jumps are before you can play them.

Example 8f:

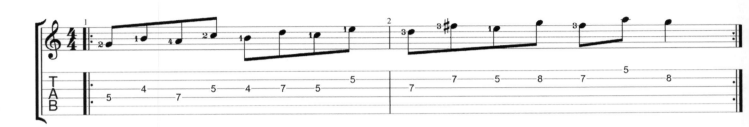

The descending version of the previous example is once again a little harder as the roll across the 7th fret notes is technically challenging. Follow the fingering in the notation carefully and begin slowly. You can always build speed once you have the accuracy mastered.

Example 8g:

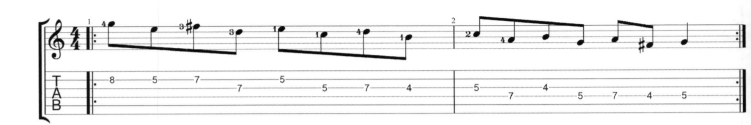

Example 8h introduces an interval skip of a fifth at the end of a descending four-note scale fragment and creates the effect of ascending melodically while playing a descending phrase. This line is quite tricky, so take it easy and make sure that you've got the sound of the pattern in your ears before speeding up. These patterns were staples of the '80s shred guitar generation and were often played at break-neck speed.

Example 8h:

Here's the descending version of the previous example. It creates a feeling of descending in pitch even though the notes of the scale are ascending. Again, the jump of a fifth will challenge you, but you'll quickly learn how to add melodic jumps and interest to otherwise scalic lead guitar lines.

Example 8i:

Finally, here's a line played in intervals of a *fourth*. Because the guitar is mainly tuned in fourths, many of the notes in the phrase are on adjacent strings and this will teach you to roll your fingers across the strings to create clear, separate notes. Try to let the first note in each pair ring until the exact moment you play the second. Ensure they don't sound at the same time.

Because the second and third strings are tuned in thirds, the fingering gets quite awkward here, but I've included this exercise deliberately to challenge you. Follow the written fingering carefully, concentrate on clear notes and keep all the unused strings muted.

Fourths are a modern, angular sound and, as with thirds and fifths, they will teach you to navigate the scale in new creative ways. It's common for beginner guitarists to play lots of stepwise scale ideas when they first start playing melodies. If you can build in intervallic jumps you'll be one step ahead of the game.

Example 8j:

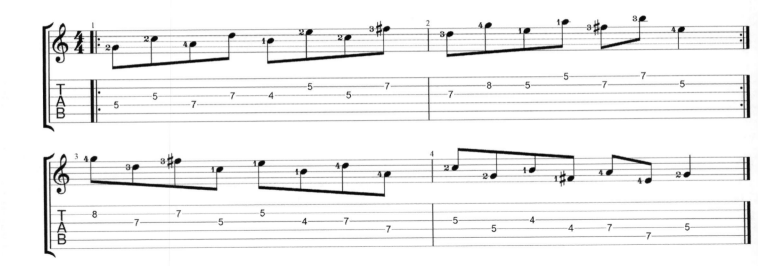

Accuracy is the name of the game in this chapter. Ensure you can play each exercise perfectly before trying to speed up.

In the next chapter we will take a break from playing single note lines and do some work to improve your rhythm and strumming of chords.

Chapter Nine: Strumming

I make clear to all my private students that I am not a 'theory first' teacher. I prefer to get hands-on and have them making music as soon as possible. The one exception to this is in the way I teach rhythm and strumming.

Your strumming hand (normally your right if you're right-handed) only has two useful directions to hit the strings: *up* and *down*. When you understand why certain strums are *ups* and others are *downs,* you build a fundamental security with rhythm. In fact, if you practise the following method, quite soon you'll never wonder how to play a rhythm again. You'll simply hear it and replicate it instantly and unconsciously.

When we talk about rhythm in music, what we're essentially doing is breaking down a song into little chunks. That song might be a 3 minute Beatles tune or a 17 minute Rachmaninov symphony. Either way, we always arrange the chunks of rhythm the same way.

You may have heard the words *bars* and *beats* before. A beat is one pulse of a song: the distance from one click to the next on your metronome. Think of the beat as a one-syllable word.

One beat of a piece of music looks like this:

♩

This note is called a **'Quarter Note'** as you can fit four of them in a bar, i.e., four 1/4 notes = 1 bar.

A bar is a *container* for the beats, and at this stage we will normally have four beats in each bar. An empty bar of music looks like this:

The 4/4 at the start tells us that there are 4 beats in the bar.

If we fill the bar with quarter notes it looks like this:

This is a whole load of preamble to get to one very simple rule:

Every time you see a ♩, you play a down strum.

Down strums are always on the beat, so if you're counting 1, 2, 3, 4 as in previous chapters, every time you say a number you strum downwards on guitar.

Look at and listen to **Example 9a:**

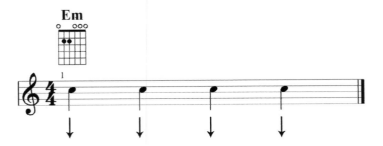

Set your metronome to play at 60 beats per minute, then play a down strum on each click while holding down the chord of E minor.

Try the same idea with A minor:

Example 9b:

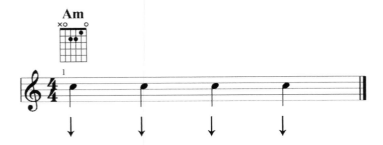

While this is a great method for developing good solid rhythm, music would be extremely dull if all our rhythms were like this.

One way to add interest is to double up on each quarter (1/4) note. In other words, imagine splitting each 1/4 note in half. This gives us 8 notes in the bar, and these are imaginatively called *1/8* or *eighth* notes.

On its own, an 1/8th note looks like this:

But when we put two of them next to each other, we join up their tails:

In other words, in music, instead of seeing two 1/8th notes written like this:

♪ ♪ you would always see them written like this: ♫

You can see that two 1/8th notes take the same amount of time to play as one 1/4 note. So...

takes the same amount of time to play as,

That is the end of the mathematics, I promise!

As you can see in the previous example, when we play 1/8th notes, our down strum is still in exactly the same place. All we need to do is squeeze in an up strum between each one. This up strum should be *exactly* in the middle of each down.

On paper it looks like this:

Example 9c:

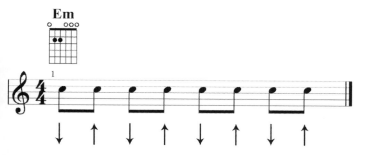

Set your metronome to 60 beats per minute and begin by playing just a down strum on each click. When you're ready, add up strums in the middle of each down. Count out loud '1 and 2 and 3 and 4 and ', etc.

Listen to the audio example to help you.

Try the same idea with other chords like D Major, shown below.

Example 9d:

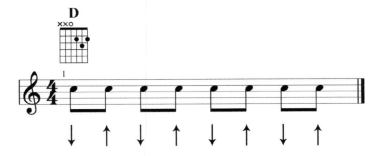

While we have added interest to our playing by adding more strums, music would be very repetitive if this was the only rhythm we ever played. To add further variety, let's learn to combine 1/4 notes and 1/8th notes.

Look at **Example 9e:**

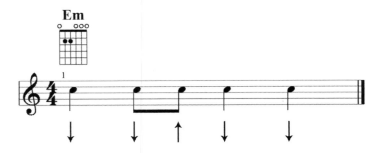

Beat 1 is a down strum, **beat 2** is a 'down-up', **beat 3** is a down strum, as is **beat 4.**

Before you play, set the metronome on 60 bpm and say out loud:

One. Two and Three. Four. Down. Down-Up Down. Down.

Say it in time, rhythmically and confidently. Saying the rhythm out loud really helps your brain to process what it needs to do to strum the rhythm in time.

When you're ready, strum the rhythm confidently. Don't worry about any buzzes in your fretting hand. Ignore them – we're only focusing on strumming.

When you're happy with the above, try the next idea.

Example 9f:

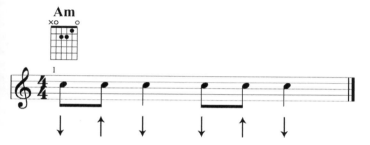

Say out loud *"One and Two. Three and Four. Down Up Down. Down Up Down."*

If it helps, you might want to think *jin gle bells jin gle bells.*

Throughout any rhythm you play on the guitar, the strumming hand never stops moving. It is constantly moving up and down in time. Downward movements are on the beats, upward movements are between the beats. This keeps you in time, like a little built-in conductor. To create rhythms, all we do is sometimes hit the strings and sometimes miss them.

Here are some other rhythms to practice:

Example 9g:

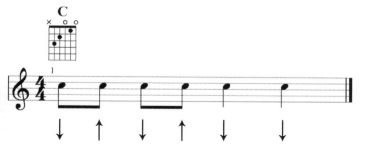

Down-Up Down-Up Down. Down.

Example 9h:

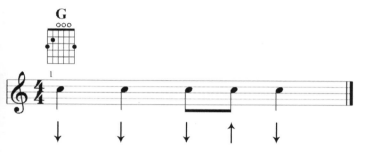

Down. Down. Down-Up Down.

With each rhythm, remember to keep your strumming hand moving down and up all the time. To play a 1/4 note, simply don't strike the guitar on the up strum.

More Interesting Rhythms

The simplest and most common way to add energy to your rhythm playing is to miss out strumming some down beats. To teach you this idea, we need to introduce a new musical symbol. It is an 1/8th note *rest* and looks like this: ⅄

This rest simply means *silence* or 'don't strum'. It will always be seen in combination with a strummed quarter note so that together they add up to one beat, like this: ⅄ ♪

Before, when we played the rhythm ♪♪ , the strumming pattern was *Down Up*. With the rhythm ⅄ ♪ , we *miss out the down strum* but *still play the up strum*.

To make this easier, always keep moving the strumming hand as if you are going to play the down strum, but simply *miss the strings*. This will keeps you in time.

In other words, the strumming hand is going up and down constantly, but *does not make contact* with the strings on the down strum. This is shown in the notation below by the grey arrow.

To practise this idea, study the following.

Example 9i:

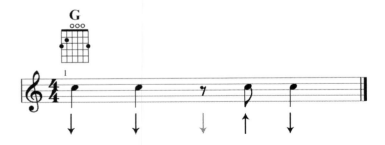

Say out loud: "Down. Down. Miss Up Down".

Next, try holding down an E minor chord while you strum this rhythm. Remember to keep the strumming hand moving all the time, miss the strings on the down strum of beat 3, but make contact on the up strum of beat '3 and'.

This is tricky at first, but incredibly important.

Once you have this idea under your fingers, try the next rhythm:

Example 9j:

Down. Down Up Miss Up Down.

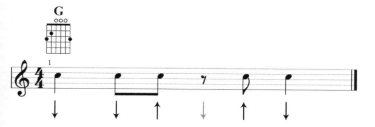

Finally, strum this:

Example 9k:

Down. Miss Up Miss Up Down.

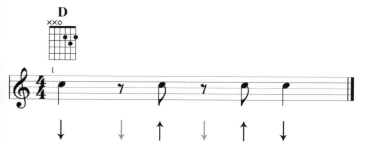

When you're comfortable with the idea of missing a down strum, transfer these rhythms to some of the chord changes given in the early chapters. There is no need to make the tasks difficult for both hands at the same time.

Try the following at 60 beats per minute.

Example 9l:

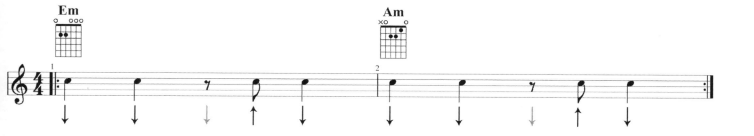

Here's one more example to spur your imagination. Spend as much time as you can mixing and matching chord changes and rhythms.

Example 9m:

Down Up Miss Up Miss Up Down.

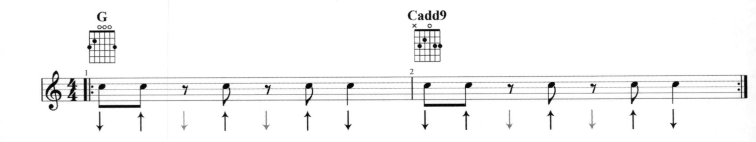

Now try making up some of your own rhythms and apply them to simple chord changes.

Chapter Ten: Slides and Bends

Sliding is a common way to change between two notes on the guitar. The idea is that you pick one fretted note and keep the pressure on the string with your finger as you slide up (or down) to the following pitch.

There are various different ways to slide notes and they all create subtly different effects. All slides are notated by a diagonal line, but there are various was of distinguishing the different techniques.

The easiest slide to play is the *legato slide*.

To play a legato slide, pick the first note and slide to the second *without* picking the string a second time. The notation for a legato slide is a diagonal (ascending or descending) line with a *slur* written above the line.

To play a legato slide, pick the first note then slide up to the second note without picking again. The first note should be held for its full rhythmic value, so there is a definite feeling of playing both pitches evenly.

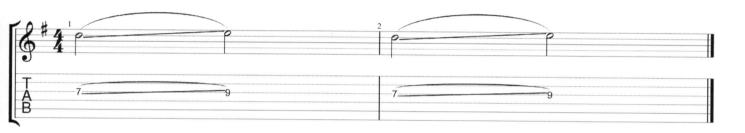

Legato slides can also be played descending.

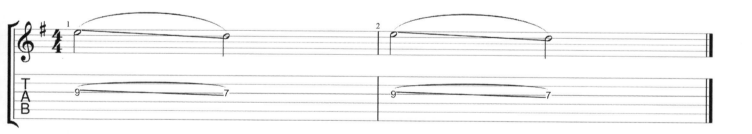

Of course, it's possible to pick the second note in the slide as well as the first. The tab notation for this slide is simply a diagonal line between the two notes, *without* the slur mark over the top.

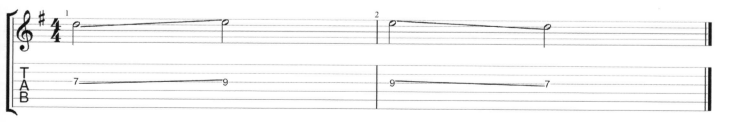

Slide Exercises

The exercises in this chapter will get you used to using slides in your playing, both for expressive effect and for seamlessly changing position on the guitar neck.

The first example is based around the central part of the A Minor Pentatonic scale. Place your first finger on the 5th fret and pick the string. Hold the note for a beat and then slide up to the 7th fret ensuring you keep enough pressure on the string to let it ring throughout. Pick the string again just as your finger leaves the 5th fret bar.

Only move your finger at the end of the beat so the whole value of the note sounds, and move your finger quickly enough so that you do *not* hear the individual notes in the middle of the slide. There should be a smooth *glissando* from the 5th to the 7th fret. Listen to the audio if you are unsure.

In the second bar, reverse the movement by playing the 7th fret, then picking the string again and sliding down to the 5th fret. The string should ring throughout.

Repeat the exercise several times using different fingers until you're confident you can create a smooth slide over a short distance.

Example 10a:

The next example is an extension of the previous movement and stretches it over a ten-fret slide. Play the 2nd fret with your first finger, hold for three beats, then pick and slide smoothly and firmly up the neck to the 12th fret. The slower you move your hand, the more individual notes you'll hear as you ascend the neck. If you go too slowly it'll sound like running your finger down a piano keyboard. Aim for a smooth, rapid glide between the notes. Repeat this idea descending in the second bar and try each movement with different fingers.

Example 10b:

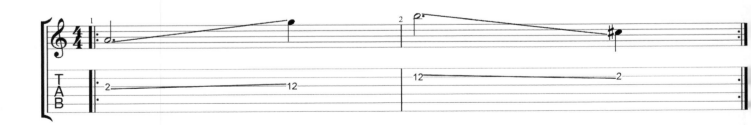

Example 10c shows how slides can be used to make a blues phrase come alive and introduces a couple of new slide movements. The first is the "slide from nowhere" and is shown by the short diagonal line before the first note. You'll notice that there is no starting point for this slide so you can experiment by sliding different distances before the picking the 7th fret.

To begin, try placing your third finger on the 6th fret and begin sliding up to the 7th *just as* you pick the string. Repeat the movement from the 5th fret, and then try starting from the 2nd fret. The further you slide, the more pronounced the effect will be. Listen to the audio to hear how it should sound.

The slide between the 7th and 9th fret is a legato slide, so you only pick the 7th fret and slide to the 9th *without* picking it. Ensure that you let the note ring fully as it's easy to let it die without the second pick.

There's a picked slide crossing the bar from the 10th to the 13th fret and back. Use your third finger and pick the 10th fret, hold it for the 1/8th note, then pick again and slide to the 13th. Hold the 13th fret for a beat then pick and slide back to the 10th. Use your first finger on the 8th fret and then pick and slide back up to the 10th.

As with the beginning of the line, this lick ends with a "slide *to* nowhere". Let the 10th fret ring and, without picking it again, slide your finger down towards the headstock of the guitar. As you relax your finger on the slide, the note will fade out beautifully.

Example 10c:

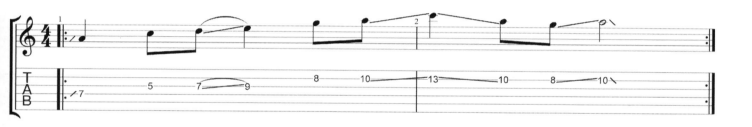

At first glance, Example 10d might look like a row of picked slides, but look again! When there are multiple legato slides (or hammer-ons and pull-offs as you'll see in the next chapter) the legato line is written over the *whole phrase*.

Use your first finger to play the first note on the 3rd fret and pick the string quite firmly. Slide up to the 5th, 7th, and 8th frets and so on *without picking* the string again, but don't forget to hold each fretted note for it's full 1/8th note value. The trick here is to use a slightly jerky wrist movement as you slide, as this adds a bit of energy to the note and helps it to ring. Listen to the audio and practise this exercise with each finger. With a little practice you should be able to keep the note ringing right up and down the scale.

Example 10d:

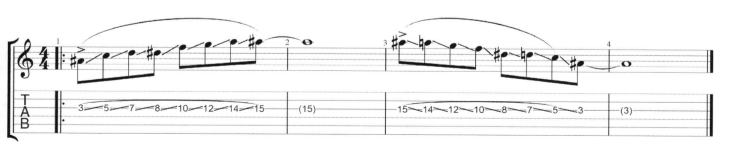

Example 10e is a similar idea to the previous one, but this time you're sliding through the scale in thirds. Pick the 3rd fret, slide up to the 7th, down to the 5th, up to the 8th etc. This will take quite a lot of stamina to perform correctly so you may need to practise this exercise in short stages. Remember to use the slightly jerky wrist action to give the note a bit of energy as you arrive at each fret.

Example 10e:

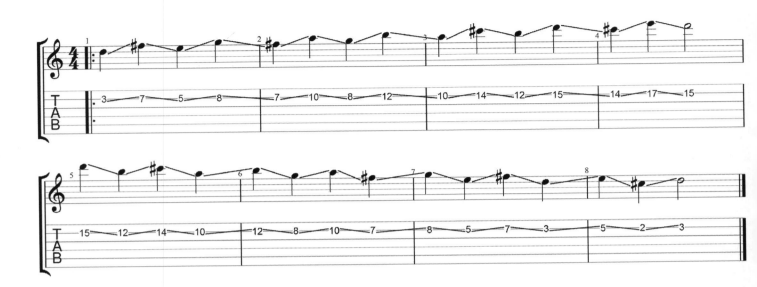

Bending Exercises

One of the most common and unique techniques used by guitar players is the bend. Bends are a great way to change pitch smoothly between a lower and a higher note. To execute a bend, you need to physically bend the string up in pitch by pushing it up the fretboard.

The amount you bend the note can be anything from less than a semitone, right up to two or more tones. The further you bend the string the higher the pitch becomes.

In tab, a bend is shown by curved line with an arrow. In the following example the note on the 7th fret of the third string (D) is bent up one tone, until it sounds exactly like the note on the 9th fret (E).

The word "full" is written above the bend to indicate that the note should be raised by a full tone.

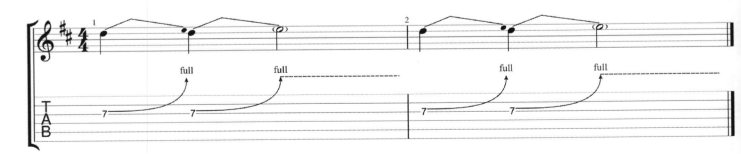

The easiest way to learn to bend is by using your third finger to fret the note and supporting it with the first and second fingers lined up on the string behind for added strength and control. Placing three fingers on the string is much stronger than using just one.

The distance you need to bend the note is always written above the arrow. The other common distance to bend a note is a 1/2 tone (semitone):

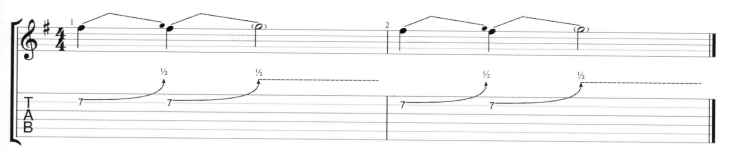

Semitone bends are easier than whole tone bends simply because you don't have to move the string as far and it is a bit easier on your fingers to begin with.

The most important thing to be aware of when bending is *intonation*. This means that each bend should be perfectly in tune. There's nothing that gives away an amateur player more quickly than an out of tune bend. Luckily, the following exercises are designed to help you learn to bend perfectly in tune, every time.

It is vital to learn to bend accurately with each finger, and your 2nd, 3rd and 4th fingers should all be capable of executing a whole tone bend.

To bend a note on the guitar you must always support the bending finger with any spare fingers below it. In other words, if you are bending a note on the 3rd string, 7th fret with your 3rd finger, your 2nd finger (if not also your 1st) should also be on the string to add power and control.

The idea behind the following is to play a reference note, descend the string a few frets and then bend perfectly back up to the reference. Treat this as an aural example: you are listening for the bent note to sound exactly like the reference pitch.

Try the following three examples with different fingers on each bend. Go through each line four times. First, bend with your 1st finger, then your 2nd etc. Don't worry about bending with your 1st finger for the tone-and-a-half bends – it is unnecessary to develop that kind of power right now.

Example 10f: Semitone bends

Example 10g: Tone bends

A pre-bend is essentially a bend in reverse. You bend the note to the desired pitch before picking it and releasing the bend. Pre-bends are notated like this:

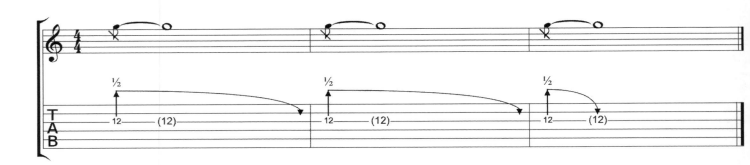

To practice this expressive technique, repeat the previous two exercises and modify them to include pre-bends in the following way.

Example 10h: Semitone pre-bends

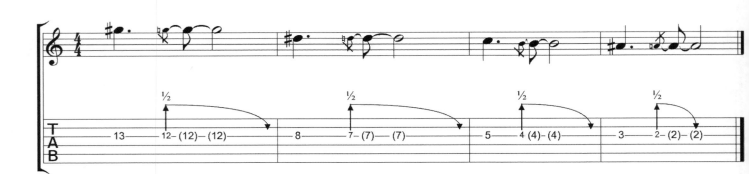

Unison bends are formed when you play two notes together on adjacent strings. The higher note is normally not bent, while the lower note is bent up to sound identical to the higher one. Jimi Hendrix and Jimi Page both made great use of this technique.

These bends are quite difficult to execute on a Floyd Rose tremolo and will always be slightly out of tune due to the nature of the mechanism, but with a bit of vibrato, intonation errors can be covered slightly.

Use your first and third fingers to play this unison bend exercise.

Example 10i: Unison bends

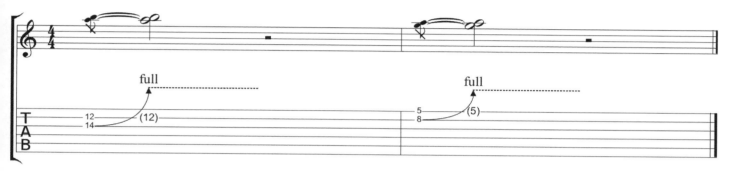

A *double-stop* is simply the act of playing two notes at the same time. A double-stop bend is when you bend both notes. This is a common technique in blues and rock guitar playing.

To play a double-stop bend, lay your finger flat with your fingernail pointing towards you. Barre your finger across two adjacent strings. To bend the notes, rotate your wrist to pull both strings downwards.

Example 10j:

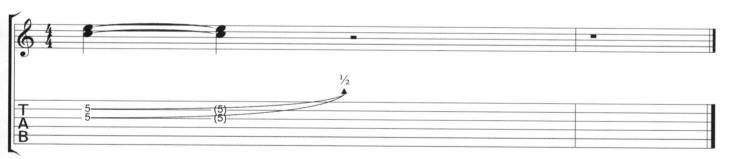

Try these all over the neck.

Chapter Eleven: Hammer-Ons and Pull Offs

A hammer-on is performed by picking a note then hammering a finger onto a note on the same string that's higher in pitch. The sign for a hammer-on is a short, curved line called a *slur* between the lower and higher pitched notes. You'll sometimes see the annotation "H/O" written above the line, but not always, so often you need to pay attention to the markings on the tab.

To perform the following hammer-on, use your first finger to play the 7th fret on the third string. Pick the note normally and hammer your *third* finger down onto the 9th fret *without picking* the string again. The secret is to hammer with the very tip of your finger, not the soft pad. Allow the second note to ring.

Hammer-on Exercises

The examples in this section will quickly develop the strength and stamina in your fretting hand and teach you to play smooth, fluid legato lines with ease.

The first example mirrors the ideas in Chapter Two, but this time you are only going to pick the first note in each group of four. Play the ascending sequence twice on each string using the one-finger-per-fret rule. The goal is to pick the first note and hammer on with sequential fingers while keeping the volume of each note the same as the picked note. You'll find that your volume naturally dies as you hammer with the weaker fingers, so don't be afraid to overdo it at first to learn the movement. Aim for power and volume before developing control.

Example 11a:

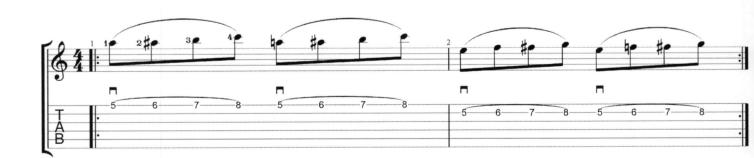

The next exercise ascends the *chromatic scale* on the guitar and your hand position must adjust one fret downwards each time you change string. What's challenging about this exercise is that your fretting hand starts out stretched across the guitar neck. This flattens your fingers and puts a bit of strain on the tendons in the hand making the hammer-ons slightly tougher to play. Try to keep a slight curve in your fingers throughout and only pick the first note on each string.

Example 11b:

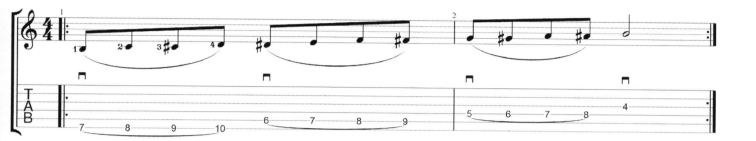

OK, are you ready for a challenge? This exercise was the beginning of a sequence taught to me by my old teacher, Shaun Baxter. The idea is that there's a repeating hammer-on pattern on the fifth string on the 5th and 7th strings, while the hammer-on pattern on the 6th and 8th frets moves across the three strings.

Keep your first finger down on the 5th fret throughout the whole exercise.

Use your first finger and pick the note on the 5th fret. Hammer on to the 7th fret with your third finger.

Use your second finger and pick the 6th fret. Hammer on to the 8th fret with your little finger. (Yep, it's tough, huh?!)

Repeat the 5th – 7th hammer-on on the fifth string then play the 6th – 8th fret movement again, but this time on the sixth string. Repeat the process moving the 6th – 8th fret movement back to the fifth, and then the fourth string.

You'll find that your fingers get fatigued quite quickly, so don't do this for more than one minute a day.

Example 11c:

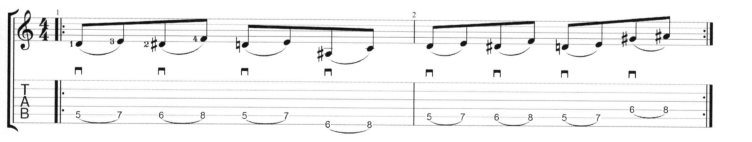

The next exercise will develop the strength and control in your third and fourth fingers. These two fingers are always weaker and require some work to bring them up to the same level as the first and second.

Use the one-finger-per-fret rule to play the following exercise and pay attention to where the picks occur on each beat. Once again, aim for power and volume before focusing on accuracy, but try to land the hammer-on on to the tip of each finger.

Example 11d:

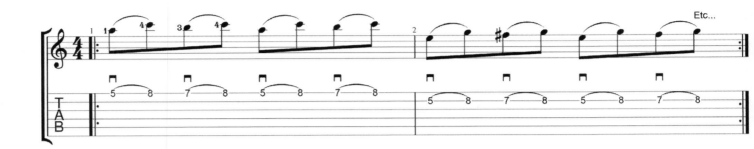

It's possible to play very quickly on the guitar using legato techniques because our picking hand has to do much less work, so let's move on to some hammer-on patterns that develop your three-note-per string scale playing and see how that works in practice.

This exercise divides the A Major scale into one-string sections and covers the three most common fingering patterns used on guitar. The idea is to play the three notes on each string with hammer-ons before returning to rest on the first note of the pattern. This is a wonderful exercise to build speed and I might even suggest that this is one of the few exercises in which it's OK to prioritise speed over rhythmic accuracy – *at first!* Just see how fast you can play the three-note segments before returning to the first note.

Gradually work your way across the scale and up the guitar neck and you'll discover an important way to play the major scale. Isolate the notes on each string and practise them as individual exercises to master these essential patterns.

As always, pay attention to the fingering instructions in the notation and play along with a metronome when you're ready to build your rhythmic accuracy.

Example 11e:

Pull-Off Exercises

It's probably no surprise, but a pull-off is the exact opposite of a hammer-on. You pick a note and pull your finger off to sound a lower pitched note.

A pull-off is again shown by a curved line over a note and looks identical to that of a hammer-on. Sometimes you'll see the letters "P/O" over the notes, but if that's not there, you must look at the pitches themselves to see whether the music calls for a hammer-on or pull off.

If the pitch of the notes ascends, use a hammer-on.

If the pitch of the notes descends, use a pull-off.

In the following figure, place your third finger on the 9th fret of the third string, and *also* place your first finger on the 7th fret of the same string.

Pick the 9th fret note and pull the third finger off (down, towards the floor) to sound the note on the 7th fret without picking the string again. Your third finger should act as a "mini pick" on your fretting hand and you must be careful not to catch the second string as you pull-off towards the floor.

Let the note on the 7th fret ring out cleanly.

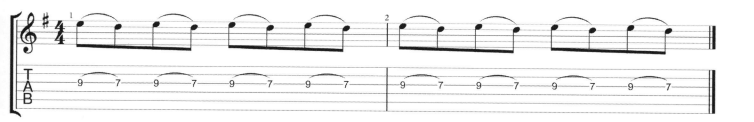

The first exercise is a descending chromatic movement that builds your control and volume. Place *all* four fingers on each fret before playing anything.

Pick the 8th fret and pull your fourth finger off the string and down towards the floor. Repeat this movement with the third and second fingers to end up on the 5th fret with the first finger. Pay attention to your rhythm and volume; each pull-off should be as loud as the picked note and should be played in even 1/8th notes.

Play along with the audio example because it's very easy to rush pull-offs and play out of time. The most important thing of all is to make sure your fingers don't catch the adjacent string as you pull your finger off, otherwise you'll create a lot of unwanted notes. Try playing these examples through an amp with a little bit of overdrive so you can hear any errors more clearly.

Example 11f:

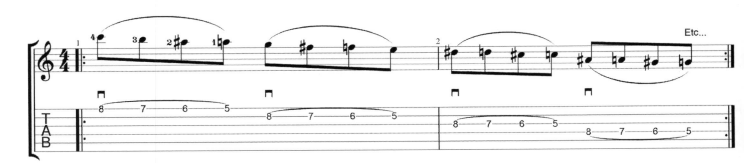

Example 11g will develop your strength and fluency with faster pull-offs by forcing you to switch fingers every bar. It's important that you listen carefully and lock in with the rhythm of the audio example. The triplets are easily rushed when you play pull-offs so be sure to stay in time.

Use the one-finger-per-fret rule to play the example using the third finger to play the 7th fret in the first bar and the second finger to play the 6th in bar two.

Example 11g:

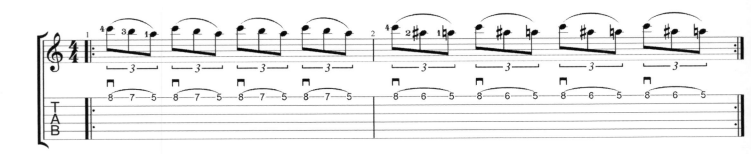

Now let's combine these legato pull-offs with a few picks. As with the economy picking concept in Chapter Three, the picks occur every time you change strings. The melody of the line is a descending four-note pattern that you've seen before, but here the picks fall in unusual places to create an interesting accent to the phrase.

As I've said before, these exercises are all about staying in time, but for the moment I want you to focus on the *volume* of the pull-off before focusing on the rhythm. The truth is that weak pull-offs sound terrible so building the finger strength is priority. When you can play the pull-offs with the same power as the picked notes, start focusing carefully on your rhythm.

Example 11h:

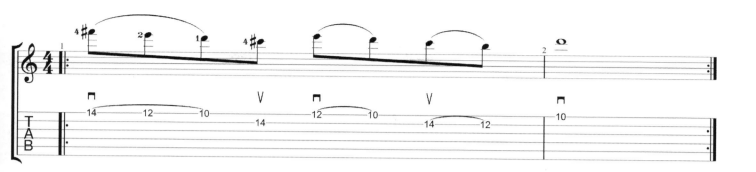

So far all the pull-off movements we've studied have been played on fretted notes, but it's important to learn how to pull-off onto open strings. It actually feels quite different to play here and it's easy for unwanted noises to slip in due to the different tensions and greater string vibration at the low end of the neck.

Example 11i is built around a descending pattern using the E Minor Pentatonic scale on the open strings of the guitar. Pick each fretted note and pull off your finger down towards the floor to sound the open string. However, you need to be accurate here because it's very easy to accidentally catch an adjacent string with your finger as you make the pull-off motion. Try to dig into the string slightly and move the finger off the string diagonally so that it misses the string above.

Example 11i:

Similar to Example 11e, the final exercise in this chapter develops your pull-off skills with the most common three shapes used to play melodies on the neck. Pick the first and final notes on each string (although you can hammer-on the final one if you're feeling brave) and focus on playing a loud, in-time triplet.

The pattern on the top two strings builds your first, third and fourth fingers.

The middle strings builds your first second and fourth fingers.

The lowest strings work your first, second and fourth fingers.

As with the hammer-ons, the further you reach over the guitar neck the more difficult the exercise becomes so try to keep a gentle curve in your fingers and play on their tips. Isolate the patterns on each string and work on them individually to make sure you're not accidentally hitting adjacent strings as you pull off.

Example 11j:

The exercises in this chapter will prepare you for any patterns or shapes you come across and you can apply the principles in these examples in any context to create your own set of finger workouts. Remember, volume, clarity and rhythm are the goals with any kind of legato practice. Always work in small bursts and speed up gradually with a metronome.

Conclusion

Well, there we have it! If you've worked through this book you should be well on your way to building great technique and a strong foundation in the basics of soloing on guitar. The key now is healthy practice and reinforcement of the good habits you're building.

As I've mentioned throughout the book, these kind of technical exercises shouldn't really account for much more than 1/3rd of any practice session and as a beginner you should always prioritise learning actual songs and making music over technique building. As you progress as a guitarist, you will find that there are times in your development that you want to immerse yourself in technique practice, but for now, learning songs and solos is the best way to build your skills. If you hit a technical roadblock while learning a song, that's the time to get into targeted exercises to improve whichever technique may be lacking.

As you progress, there are some books you may wish to invest in. In order of difficulty I suggest you check out:

• The Guitar Finger Gym

• Complete Technique for Modern Guitar

And for the really brave shredders among you,

• Neo-Classical Speed Strategies for Guitar

All of these books from Fundamental Changes will greatly heighten your skill on the guitar and leave you more able to tackle those difficult solo passages.

It's always useful to play a bit of blues because it's a universal language of music. Check out my series of books, The Complete Guide to Playing Blues Guitar to immerse yourself in this important genre.

Above all, spend your practice time learning the music you love, whether it's a three-chord pop song or crazy jazz fusion. There's so much happiness to be found in music it's a shame to spend your life practising exercises. The exercises only come into the equation when playing the music you love is a little beyond your current ability.

So, what are you waiting for? Grab up your guitar and go for it!

Have fun!

Joseph!

P.S., Reviews are like gold dust for writers. If you like this book, please help us spread the word and leave a review on Amazon. Just think of all those lovingly crafted and notated examples… all the painstakingly recorded audio and the carefully worded explanations… Surely that's worth two minutes of your time to help other people make a smart choice for their music education!

Thanks ☺

Printed in Poland
by Amazon Fulfillment
Poland Sp. z o.o., Wrocław